"The wisdom we really need may not be the wisdom we typically seek. This book will challenge your assumptions, open new windows of understanding, and realign your relationships. Filtered through the life experience of a veteran pastor and renewal leader, the practical truths in *The Prayer God Loves to Answer* will connect you to the life of Christ to empower you for lasting life-change."

Mark Batterson, *New York Times* bestselling author of *The Circle Maker* and lead pastor of National Community Church

"Daniel Henderson is a seasoned saint, a serious follower of Christ, and a profoundly humble man of God. Whenever he joins me on the show, I look forward to a thoughtful, engaging, deeper-life kind of conversation. That's why I'm thrilled about his latest book, *The Prayer God Loves to Answer*. He's written a timely word for the church and for those who know they need wisdom only found in Jesus, the source of all wisdom. I pray we can put as much thought into reading these words as Daniel put into writing them. Our world needs God's wisdom. Desperately. May God equip and empower you as you read!"

Susie Larson, talk radio host, national speaker, and author of *Your Powerful Prayers*

"Foolish choices are ruining the fabric of our nation and our lives. What we need is more of Jesus, more of his wisdom, more of his truth. Daniel Henderson delivers just that. *The Prayer God Loves to Answer* is a journey for wisdom and a map to some of God's greatest highlights along the way."

Lance Hahn, senior pastor of Bridgeway Christian Church and author of *How to Live in Fear—Mastering the Art of Freaking Out*

"Anyone who has believed the gospel must also learn to apply it to every area of their lives. With careful exposition and relentless application, Daniel Henderson explains the implications of the good news of Christ in one of the most important aspects of our journey—our everyday relationships. You won't see your relationships the same again after reading this book, and you'll be equipped to pray for much-needed wisdom in a fresh and life-transforming way."

Brian Bloye, senior pastor of West Ridge Church and coauthor of *It's Personal*

"I start every single day by asking God to fill me with his divine wisdom. I have learned through the years that I can do nothing without him, and I even mess that up if he doesn't fill me with wisdom. And yet, the moment I started reading Daniel's book, I immediately refocused my whole view of wisdom: It's not about me, it's all about Jesus. Every Christian who wants to grow deeper in their faith, who wants to be more fruitful and discerning and experience an abundant life, must read this book."

Karen Covell, producer and founding director of *The Hollywood Prayer Network*

"As a pastor and biblical counselor, I know there is no more practical guide to engaging people with the wisdom of God than through Gospel-centered prayer. In a generation of nothing more than 'give-me' prayers, it is time we seek God for more than just results, and gain perspective and wisdom for life's daily challenges. Daniel Henderson has done it again! This book is a guide for taking your eye off of yourself and gaining the greater gift God wants to give you through prayer: more of himself!"

Josh Weidmann, senior pastor, Grace Chapel, author of *Honest to God*, and host of www.joshweidmann.com

TRANSFORMING

Wisdom

formerly published as
The Prayer God Loves to Answer

Books by Daniel Henderson

In The 6:3 Discipleship Guidepost Series

Transforming Prayer
The Deeper Life
Transforming Presence
Transforming Wisdom

Available at strategicrenewal.com

Prayzing!
How to Pray in a Crisis
Fresh Encounters

TRANSFORMING *Wisdom*

How Unleashing Christ's Wisdom Changes Everything

DANIEL HENDERSON

Building 6:3 Disciples
Becoming 6:4 Leaders
Believing for a 6:7 Awakening

STRATEGIC RENEWAL

Published by Strategic Renewal
www.strategicrenewal.com

Printed in the United States of America

ISBN 978-0-7642-1833-0

To Heather Rose

Our cherished daughter
whose tender heart and willing obedience to Jesus
has filled our lives with deepest joy.
Now, as a wife and mother,
she continues to beautifully honor her Lord.

Contents

Foreword

When I was in my early twenties, a friend came to me and said, "I'm dating this guy who just told me we can't talk about the possibility of marriage until we both memorize the book of Proverbs. What should I do?" she asked, astonishment showing in her great big eyes.

"Well, maybe you should memorize it!" I responded. "In fact, I'd like to do it with you."

So the three of us started working on memorizing the book of Proverbs. As it turned out, my friend ended up marrying someone else, but what a wonderful journey those months turned out to be for me. A journey toward wisdom. Here are a few of the lessons I learned about wisdom in the process:

1. Wisdom provides a sense of personal security, stability, and well-being. (Proverbs 3:21–26)
2. Wisdom builds strong homes and promotes happy family relationships. (Proverbs 24:3; 10:1; 19:13)
3. Wisdom earns favor in the workplace. (Proverbs 14:35; 17:2)
4. Wisdom enables us to overcome major obstacles and opposition. (Proverbs 21:22 and 24:5; Ecclesiastes 9:18)
5. Wisdom helps us work smarter, not harder. (Ecclesiastes 10:10)
6. Wisdom exalts us before others. (Proverbs 3:35)

7. Wisdom diffuses angry people and situations. (Proverbs 29:8; 16:14)
8. Wisdom positively affects our physical health and well-being. (Proverbs 14:30; 3:7–8)
9. Wisdom provides protection. (Proverbs 2:11–16)

As I have continued to meditate on the Proverbs over the years, I have found myself asking, "What is the essence of wisdom?"

Wisdom is really learning to see all of life from God's point of view—seeing every season, circumstance, and situation of life as he sees it. We have to ask God to help us see life as he sees it because we can't see what He sees and we don't know what he knows.

Wisdom is orienting and ordering every area of our lives around God, his ways, and his Word. It's aligning everything in our lives—our thoughts, speech, relationships, work, worship, play, health, diet—around God. It is living life with the recognition that our lives revolve around God as the earth revolves around the sun. It is living life in sync with the Creator of the universe.

Wisdom is always asking the question "What pleases God?" Does it please God when I talk this way or when I treat my employee or employer that way? Does it please God when I spend money on this item? It's continually checking in with God—about everything.

Wisdom is connecting the dots between cause and effect in our lives. We make certain choices, and those choices have effects. Wisdom helps us to connect those dots to see the relationship between certain behaviors and their outcomes. It's realizing that every choice, every action has consequences, and we reap what we sow. The wise person always thinks about the outcome of his or her way of life.

Sadly, so many people I meet today are metaphorically running red lights and driving recklessly in their lives. They are living without regard for the laws of God and then wondering why their lives are falling apart.

God is saying, "You ran the stoplights; you weren't wearing a seat belt; you were driving recklessly. I'm not mad at you. But I love you enough that I'm going to put on the brakes and bring circumstances into your life so you can see your life from wisdom's point of view."

We need to move past the symptoms of our problems and deal with the root causes. We need to ask God to help us connect the dots between our sinful choices and the consequences in our lives, families, and communities. We need to ask forgiveness, make things right, and cry out for his grace to live a life grounded in the wisdom that comes from him.

What the world considers wise is invariably foolishness to God. Conversely, what God considers wise is generally foolishness to the world.

You can walk in the world's wisdom and be foolish to God, or you can walk in God's wisdom and be considered foolish by the world. But you can't have it both ways.

As Christians, I fear we spend far too much time trying to fit into this world, trying to be esteemed, accepted, and applauded by the world for thinking as the world thinks. But if we do that, we're setting ourselves up to be fools in God's eyes.

This book on wisdom is yet another wonderful resource for the church. Daniel draws on decades of experience in leading churches to seek the Lord through worship-based prayer rooted in the wisdom of the Scriptures.

At the end of each chapter Daniel provides a guide for discussion and prayer. This supplementary material is a great springboard for small groups and congregations to pray in accordance with wisdom.

The ancient Proverb could not be more relevant for life in the twenty-first century: "There is a way that appears to be right, but in the end it leads to death" (Proverbs 14:12).

By God's grace, this book will help believers live and walk in God's wisdom and in Christ, who is the Wisdom of God!

Nancy DeMoss Wolgemuth
Author and Teacher/Host of *Revive Our Hearts*

Preface

In the course of the Christian life, certain passages of Scripture grip your mind, arrest your heart, alter your life, and never let you go. For decades, this has been my experience with James 3:17–18.

> But the wisdom from above is first pure, then peaceable, gentle, open to reason, full of mercy and good fruits, impartial and sincere. And a harvest of righteousness is sown in peace by those who make peace.

As a pastor, I have preached this passage and seen life-changing results. As a counselor, I have challenged struggling couples and discouraged believers to experience the help and healing grace of these truths. As an author, I have now been enriched to quarry and reapply these insights during a season of personal challenge. As a Christ-follower, these memorized principles have surfaced countless times to change my attitudes, words, and actions. There are no biblical passages I have quoted to myself in times of relational challenge or attitudinal meltdown more than James 3:17–18.

Someone asked me the other day, "How long did it take you to write this book?" My answer: "A lifetime." Yes, there were months of concentrated typing and editing. But these hours were preceded by decades of repeated encounter and encouragement. Honestly, these verses are to me more profound and practical today than ever. Like a treasure chest with no bottom, it seems the more I dig, the more I delight.

My prayer is that you will not just read this book, but that you will experience it. I pray that a true gospel-oriented approach to wisdom will keep you from ever reading the Bible in the same old way.

At my ordination many years ago, I requested we sing the classic hymn "More About Jesus." The third verse reads:

> More about Jesus in his Word,
> Holding communion with my Lord;
> Hearing his voice in ev'ry line,
> Making each faithful saying mine.[1]

I pray that in the coming years, every biblical insight you contemplate about New Testament wisdom will lead you to cry out, "More, more about Jesus!" and as a result, your prayers will be elevated to a new level of trust and expectation.

At the end of each chapter you will find a section titled "Ready to Receive." These simple points of practical application are designed to help you embrace a greater awareness and expectation for experiencing God's answer to your prayer for wisdom. God is eager to impart his wisdom. We must be willing and responsive in receiving it.

I've often said the best way to apply God's Word is to pray it. To that end, I have also provided a prayer response for each chapter. Whether in private or group prayer, I hope you will engage these guides to bring this Christ-centered wisdom to the core of your soul. Each prayer is based on a passage of Scripture using the pattern Jesus gave us in the Lord's Prayer. (An overview of this prayer approach can be found in appendix 1.) I also invite you to use the discussion questions near the end of the book to further apply what you read to the fabric of your thoughts and everyday life. These can also be used for small-group discussions.

Now, let's begin. The prayer for gospel wisdom is a prayer God loves to answer. Being so generous in wisdom, he loves to hear your voice. When you cry out to him with your eyes on Jesus and pray according to his Word, I suspect you will sense his response: "I'm so glad you asked!"

Introduction: Wisdom Within

> Who is wise and understanding among you?
>
> James 3:13

> The road to significance is not straight. There is a curve called Failure, a loop called Perplexity, speed bumps called Friends, red lights called Enemies, caution lights called Family. You will have flats called Trials. But, if you have a spare called Faith, an engine called Grace, insurance called Truth, fuel called Love, and a driver called Jesus, you will make it to a place called Significance.
>
> Source Unknown (adapted)

The summary of my story is this: I can't make it through this life on my own. Try as I can to be self-sufficient, capable, and effective, I come up short. In so many ways, though, I'm sure my story is your story, is all of our stories. Whether we review salient scenes of our past or ponder a snapshot of the present moment, we must ultimately admit that the demands, decisions, and relationships of everyday life are more than we can fix or control.

That's why we need wisdom. The good news? Christ is ready and willing to give us wisdom beyond ourselves—beyond our human reason, our best education, our natural instincts, and our accumulated experiences.

Do you remember a time when you were in a relationship that was at the boiling point, or picking up the pieces of one that seemed broken beyond repair? I do. Have you ever been in agony over a personal failure, feeling distraught about how the next chapter of life might unfold? I have. Can you think of a time when you didn't know how to help your hurting child, or you advised a devastated friend, or called a wandering family member back to faith? I can. Will you encounter a crisis in your health, a crushing of your heart, or a crossroads in your future that will bring you to your knees in unreserved desperation? I know I will. My best guess is that you will too.

Whoever you are, wherever you are, whatever you have done, are doing, or will do—you need wisdom. Regardless of your age, your race, your regrets, your hopes, your fears, your doubts, or your faith—you need wisdom.

You may be single, married, lonely, bored, overloaded, or overlooked. Perhaps you are sick, healthy, depressed, or overjoyed. You might be poor, rich, educated, or not. Maybe you are at the top of your game or can't seem to find your game. You need wisdom.

It doesn't matter if you have failed, succeeded, or simply feel average. Regardless of your personality, perceptions, or principles—you need wisdom. You may be a mother, father, son, daughter, teacher, preacher, engineer, architect, administrator, student, retiree, or CEO. You need wisdom.

You need wisdom that is right, reliable, and relevant. You need wisdom to pilot your daily decisions and point you to your destiny. You need wisdom to shape your thoughts and govern your emotions. You need wisdom to understand yourself and to get along with the people you love—and especially the ones you don't.

What Kind of Wisdom?

Just what is this prized treasure called wisdom? Some think of it as the trait of a godly parent or a seasoned grandparent. Perhaps you picture an insightful friend or helpful counselor. Others call to mind some type of religious sage, university professor, or a local church pastor. You might think of the teachings of a bestselling author or the principles of a renowned historical figure.

Merriam-Webster tells us wisdom is:

- "Knowledge that is gained by having many experiences in life."
- "The natural ability to understand things that most other people cannot understand."
- "Knowledge of what is proper or reasonable. Good sense or judgment."[1]

Other common definitions of wisdom include "truth applied to life" and "seeing life from God's perspective." One Bible dictionary tells us that "wisdom takes insights gleaned from the knowledge of God's ways and applies them in the daily walk."[2] Another solid description says, "Wisdom is not intellectual enlightenment but insight into the will of God and the ability to apply it to everyday life."[3] A landmark biblical description says it this way: "The fear of the Lord is the beginning of wisdom, and the knowledge of the Holy One is insight" (Proverbs 9:10).

While these definitions are all compelling, they are missing something. They talk about wisdom that can inform the mind and chart the course but may not have the power to change the heart. There remains an essential truth that is a game changer for the Christian who wants to live wisely, who needs to live wisely. This "something" is the gospel of Jesus Christ.

A Transforming Wisdom

Because of Jesus' redeeming work on the cross and the availability of his resurrection power, Christ-followers are now in a life-changing relationship with the indwelling source of the highest and best wisdom.

The gospel of Jesus Christ is not just our introduction to the Christian life. It is the essence of our Christian life. It is not just the message of Christianity. It is the meaning of Christianity. It is not just the story of Jesus. The gospel is about the sufficiency of Jesus for all things. The gospel enlightens us to understand that Christ is the one in whom is hidden "all the treasures of wisdom and knowledge" (Colossians 2:3). Jesus Christ is "the power of God and the wisdom of God" (1 Corinthians 1:24) and our "righteousness and sanctification and redemption" (1 Corinthians 1:30).

So for a Christian, the experience of wisdom is not the art of figuring it out but the adventure of following him. The pursuit of wisdom is more than comprehending concepts. It is the privilege of knowing Christ. This is experienced through abiding in him through prayer, the truth of his Word, and the indwelling of his life in our souls, like a nuclear reactor at the core of a power plant.

A Gospel Definition

Traditional thoughts on wisdom focus on filling the head with ideas that can lead to greater accomplishment. Gospel wisdom rules the heart through intimacy with Christ. This wisdom is more than prudent information to guide your next enterprise. It is power that leads to personal transformation. It is not about rules for better behavior but a relationship that changes the heart. This wisdom transcends weighty concepts that produce manageable relationships. Rather, it converts one's character in a way that can morph everything about a relationship.

Here is an attempt at a truly Christian, explicitly simple, gospel-centered definition of wisdom: **Wisdom is Jesus Christ—embraced, experienced, exemplified, and exalted in our lives and relationships.**

- *Embraced* through saving and sustaining faith in Christ's sufficiency for all things
- *Experienced* by his abiding in us and our abiding in him through prayer and God's Word
- *Exemplified* as Christ manifests his wisdom through us to influence others
- *Exalted* as the supernatural fruit of his life in us, which glorifies his name

Said another way, wisdom is the abiding life of Jesus Christ experienced in prayer, vitalizing my relationship with God, and transforming my relationships with others.

With this new understanding, everything can change. Every thought and emotion can be different. Every trial and problem can produce fresh benefits. Every role and responsibility can be more fruitful. Every relationship can bear the beauty of the life of Christ.

Our Wisdom Journey

In the following pages we will discover how wisdom brings about powerful and practical benefits. We will be warned of the destructive results of rejecting biblical wisdom. And while wisdom is vital to real-world achievement, we will discover that it ultimately results in relational authenticity. At the core of our discovery, we will delight in the amazing truth that Jesus Christ is the source of a truly transformational wisdom and the ultimate treasure for every wisdom seeker.

In part 1 of this book, we will unpack this truly revolutionary New Testament idea of wisdom, found and fulfilled in Jesus Christ and now active in you because of his indwelling life. We will see how his wisdom meets your greatest needs and the needs of others.

Part 2 will address one of the most practical and complete New Testament explanations of wisdom, described by James, the half-brother of Jesus. As you read this book you will understand how prayer is key to unleashing the wisdom of Jesus Christ. All along, you will be assured of God's delight in answering your requests for his life-changing wisdom.

The Diamond of Wisdom in Your Own Backyard

In 1870, Russell Conwell, an American Baptist minister, orator, philanthropist, and lawyer, heard a riveting story, passed on to him by an old Arab tour guide while visiting the Middle East. Eventually the story became a famous speech that Conwell delivered over six thousand times across the globe.

He recounted the story of a wealthy man named Ali Hafed, who lived not far from the River Indus. Ali "was contented because he was wealthy, and wealthy because he was contented," it was said. One day a priest visited Ali Hafed and told him about some mysterious diamonds that could produce untold wealth for the one who found them.

Pondering the diamond story, Ali "went to his bed that night a poor man," Conwell noted. "He had not lost anything, but he was poor because he was discontented, and discontented because he feared he was poor."

Soon Ali sold his farm, left his family, and traveled throughout Palestine and then to Europe searching for diamonds, which, sadly, he never discovered. Eventually his health and his wealth failed. Dejected, he cast himself into the sea and took his own life.

One day, Conwell wrote, "The man who had purchased Ali Hafed's farm found a curious sparkling stone in a stream that cut through his land. It was a diamond. Digging produced more diamonds—acres of diamonds, in fact. This, according to the parable, was the discovery of the famed diamonds of Golconda."[4]

Christ in Us

The point of the story is that we often chase after things we perceive to be of value in "other" places when they can actually be found right where we are. Wisdom is often thought of as something we acquire from other people, additional experiences, or through a popular new book. Of course, these sources can be helpful. But the best and greatest wisdom is already within us if we know Christ and abide in him.

Physically, we have profound systems at work in our body that we seldom contemplate or cherish.

- Our heart quietly and consistently pumps life-giving blood through our body.
- Our lungs instinctively infuse our system with vital oxygen.
- Our nervous system serves like electrical wiring to coordinate our actions and reactions.

- Our bones give structure and protection to the rest of our functions.
- Our muscles provide strength and movement to our desired actions.
- Our digestive organs convert food to energy and cleanse us from impurities.
- Our reproductive system allows us to generate life.

Apart from significant disease or a handicap, these physical systems provide all we need for health and optimum performance. Of course they require care, nutrition, and proper maintenance in some cases, but they are consistently functioning on our behalf.

As you think about wisdom, it is imperative that you embrace and emphasize what is already yours. Just as God's design serves our physical capacities, so his design for our life in Christ empowers our spiritual and relational potential. The truth of his life in us is constant. We must abide, attend to, and apply this reality on a daily basis.

Christ in you—the hope of glory. He is your all in all. He is wisdom in you, for you, and through you to others; all for our satisfaction, his delight, and the advancement of his gospel. Pray from this reality and for this reality every day. It is a prayer God loves to answer.

PART ONE

Best Wisdom Available

1

Wise Beyond Solomon

> Thy power created the universe from nothing; Thy wisdom has managed all its multiple concerns, presiding over nations, families, individuals.
>
> Thy goodness is boundless; all creatures wait on thee, are supplied by thee, are satisfied in thee.[1]
>
> A Puritan Prayer

> It is vitally important that we hold the truth of God's infinite wisdom as a tenet of our creed: but this is not enough. We must by the exercise of faith and by prayer bring it into the practical world of our day-by-day experience.[2]
>
> A.W. Tozer

We've all prayed earnestly to God with zealous hope that he would answer our requests. In some cases, we look back, grateful he did not comply. Perhaps we rejoice that he did. At other times, we've seen him answer clearly but not in exact acquiescence to what we asked. Some still carry the heartache of an answer that never came, at least not one that we could understand. This reminds me of a beloved prayer penned by an anonymous Civil War soldier:

I asked God for strength that I might achieve.
I was made weak that I might learn humbly to obey.
I asked God for health, that I might do greater things.
I was given infirmity that I might do better things.
I asked for riches that I might be happy.
I was given poverty, that I might be wise.
I asked for power that I might have the praise of men.
I was given weakness that I might feel the need of God.
I asked for all things that I might enjoy life.
I was given life that I might endure all things.
I got nothing that I asked for—but everything that I had
hoped for.
Almost despite myself my unspoken prayers were answered.
I am among all men most richly blessed.[3]

What a great reminder that God *does* respond to our prayers. His answers are not always aligned with what we *think* we need but always with a view to what we *really do* need.

Annual Rejection

At the risk of seeming shallow and materialistic, I must confess that most years I enter the HGTV Dream Home contest. With no exchange of money, it is not gambling. But with my daily online entry, there is often an accompanying prayer that I hope God will answer. I figure that since someone has to win, it might as well be me. Surely God knows what a good steward I would prove to be with my new luxury home that could be used for a pastors' retreat. The new car that accompanies the home would provide reliable transportation. The other associated prizes could be given to needy friends or my struggling adult children. *Lord, hear my prayer!*

God always has applied his divine filter to my earnest pleas and decided against me hitting the jackpot. Come to think of it, I've prayed a lot of prayers much like that dream house supplication—some frivolous, some thoughtful, many simply inconsequential. Most of these prayers were offered without any true assurance that God would love to answer them.

There is one prayer I can tell you that God loves to answer: the prayer for divine wisdom. How do I know this? There are many biblical reasons as to why we can classify a prayer for wisdom as the prayer God welcomes. We will see these in the next chapter. But let's start with one early illustration found in the life of King Solomon.

What an Offer!

Be honest—raw honest. If God gave you the option of asking him for anything your heart desires (yes, *anything*), what would it be? A cabin on a lake? Five million dollars in your retirement account? Healing of your terminal disease? Children who excel academically? Fame equal to Taylor Swift's? A custom Tesla Model S car? World peace?

As for me, I wouldn't mind a Rocky Mountain retreat center for pastors or a book that becomes a bestseller. I might ask for well-paying and crystal-clear career paths for my adult children or a paid-off mortgage on my home. In a carnal moment I might even ask for a full head of hair or smaller ears. Clearly, I need to be content and focus my wishbone a little higher toward heavenly concerns. The bottom line: This kind of offer from the King of the universe would definitely test our motives and reveal our true values.

It was this very offer that set the life trajectory for Solomon, notably one of the wisest humans ever. Facing the ominous assignment of succeeding his father, David, on the throne of Israel, and tasked with the holy privilege and responsibility of building the nation's first temple for the worship of Jehovah, Solomon certainly had needs.

Of course, he required support from the people, a loyal staff to help him organize the kingdom, massive provisions for the temple project, and protection from jealous relatives and zealous enemies. He was already teetering on spiritual compromise, so he could have asked for spiritual correction and a personal revival. His wish list was likely extraordinary, perhaps endless.

In spite of his pressing necessities and obvious flaws in the early days of his leadership, Solomon "loved the Lord, walking in the statutes of David his father" (1 Kings 3:3). Solomon had personally witnessed the great and steadfast love of God to David and knew this very love had now placed him on the throne, albeit through a messy process. Solomon had a front row seat watching his dad's journey, who, while very imperfect, still walked before God "in faithfulness, in righteousness, and in uprightness of heart." Knowing his inadequacy, Solomon humbly confessed, "I am but a little child. I do not know how to go out or come in" (1 Kings 3:6–7).

This is the backdrop to the answer of his heart when, by way of a nighttime dream, almighty God declared, "Ask what I shall give you." Solomon's response? "Give your servant therefore an understanding mind to govern your people, that I may discern between good and evil, for who is able to govern this your great people?" (1 Kings 3:9).

The rest, as they say, is history. In Solomon's case, the story unfolded for better and for worse, in greatness and in disaster, in humble beginnings and miserable endings. Let's start with the good news.

Blessings Unleashed

God's delight in Solomon's singular desire for wisdom brought unprecedented success. The Bible says, "God gave Solomon wisdom and understanding beyond measure, and breadth of mind like the sand on the seashore, so that Solomon's wisdom surpassed the wisdom of all the people of the east and all the wisdom of Egypt. . . . He was wiser than all other men . . . and his fame was in all the surrounding nations" (1 Kings 4:29–31). We know Solomon solved difficult problems, was sought out by distinguished royalty from other nations, and led with such political insight that Israel was at her pinnacle—united and prosperous.

Solomon's resulting wealth boggles the mind. In all likelihood, no one in history has accumulated as much gold and silver.[4] Solomon ruled Israel for forty years, and he brought in a modern equivalent of 1.1 billion dollars of gold *each year*.[5] Beyond the yearly amount of gold, we know his wealth also included:

- His inheritance from his father, King David
- Gold and silver received from the kings of Arabia, governors, and merchants

- The heavy taxes paid by the Israelites
- Tribute money from other countries and kingdoms
- Gold, silver, ivory, apes, monkeys, Ethiopians, and peacocks received every three years due from his business partnership with Hiram, king of Tyre
- Additional gifts of gold, spices, precious stones, garments, armor, horses, and mules each year

Solomon became so immensely rich that all his cups were made of gold ("none were of silver," it says in 1 Kings 10:21), and his wealth was so extraordinary that gold and silver were as common in Jerusalem as pebbles (2 Chronicles 1:15; 1 Kings 10:27).[6]

His skills in leadership resulted in the successful completion of the first temple, which became the centerpiece of Israel's worship, housing the Ark of the Covenant. This monumental task took seven years as Solomon commanded a general Jewish labor force of thirty thousand men, plus an additional seventy thousand common laborers, eighty thousand to quarry stone in the mountains, and more than three thousand to oversee them (1 Kings 5:13; 2 Chronicles 2:2).

Militarily, Solomon was a powerhouse. In describing the size of his forces, the Bible says, "Solomon also had 40,000 stalls of horses for his chariots, and 12,000 horsemen" (1 Kings 4:26). The blessing of all of this is noted, "He had peace on all sides around him. And Judah and Israel lived in safety, from Dan even to Beersheba, every man under his vine and under his fig tree, all the days of Solomon" (1 Kings 4:24–25).

The Bible also extols Solomon's practical wisdom: "He spoke of trees, from the cedar that is in Lebanon even to the hyssop that grows on the wall; he spoke also of animals and birds and creeping things and fish" (1 Kings 4:33 NASB). It seems he lectured on everything from morality to biology. Some have described Solomon as a true "Renaissance Man," one who had an enlightened view of the world around him.

But more familiar to most of us is the fact that "he also spoke 3,000 proverbs, and his songs were 1,005" (1 Kings 4:32). Some of Solomon's wisdom has been regarded as inspired Scripture and is found in two psalms (72 and 127), most of the book of Proverbs, the Song of Solomon (Song of Songs), and probably Ecclesiastes.

Proverbs is a poetic collection of moral and philosophical maxims serving as a guidebook to successful living. The Song of Solomon makes no mention of God but is a beautiful dramatic description of romantic love. And Ecclesiastes is a raw summary of the futility of all human pursuits, even wisdom, apart from knowing and honoring God. Some would say it captures the "vanity" of Solomon's many accomplishments that ultimately left him dissatisfied with life—which leads us to the dark side of his journey.

The Confounding Demise of Greatness

A mentor of mine during my college days often would remind me that "the main performance that counts is the last one." A dramatic start with a disastrous finish leaves a sour taste in the souls of all who evaluate the contributions of one's life.

We simply have to read 1 Kings 11 to realize Solomon's dreadful failure to steward his gift of wisdom for his ultimate good and God's ultimate glory. In summary, Solomon deliberately and persistently disobeyed God's prohibition against intermarrying women from pagan nations. The Bible states, "He had 700 wives, who were princesses, and 300 concubines. And his wives turned away his heart" (1 Kings 11:3). Solomon rejected the worship of God because of his own sexual lust (which was never satisfied with one or a thousand women). Undoubtedly, many of these "marriages" fulfilled a political expediency and were fueled by his growing obsession with power and prestige.

Eventually, even after two direct visitations from God warning him of his evil ways, Solomon persisted in overtly establishing pagan worship in Israel, chasing after the idols from the religions of his many wives. God tormented Solomon by raising up two foreign political adversaries and one who rebelled from within (see 1 Kings 14:14–28).

The capstone of Solomon's wretched finale was God's judgment, declaring that the kingdom of Israel would be divided after Solomon's death, with one tribe reigning in Judah to the south under his son and the other tribes existing separately in the north (1 Kings 11:9–13). In time this led to wars between the two kingdoms, weakened economies, and vulnerability against other hostile nations.

Relational Failure

It is safe to classify Solomon as a relational failure. Using God's wisdom for his own ends and void of any internal empowering of grace, Solomon's legacy unraveled in tragic proportions. One outstanding example was seen in the life of his son and successor, Rehoboam. Not only was his political leadership tragic, but his duplication of Solomon's relational misconduct prolonged the consequences of a wisdom failure.

One commentator writes,

> Rehoboam was the son of Solomon, a preoccupied father who himself grew increasingly lax about spiritual things. Rehoboam's mother was Naamah, a pagan Ammonite princess who presumably lacked any spiritual perception (1 Kings 14:21). His father's example of keeping a harem and having numerous children likewise had an impact on him. Rehoboam had 18 wives, 60 concubines, 28 sons, and 60 daughters. He spent a considerable amount of time providing living arrangements for them in the fortified cities of Judah (2 Chronicles 11:21–23).[7]

Eventually Rehoboam completely "forsook the law of the Lord, and all Israel with him" (2 Chronicles 12:1 KJV). In the end, the apostasy of Rehoboam's reign became so great that God brought judgment on the nation in the form of a foreign invasion. In the fifth year of Rehoboam's leadership, Egypt invaded Palestine with 1,200 chariots and 60,000 men (1 Kings 14:25; 2 Chronicles 12:2–3). The Bible states that this invasion was direct punishment for their sinful ways. Eventually the national treasury and the temple treasury were emptied to satisfy the demands of the Egyptians.

Scripture implies that Rehoboam's latter years were characterized by evil (2 Chronicles 12:14), and that his son and successor Abijam "walked in all the sins which his father did before him" (1 Kings 15:3). Spiritual and relational collapse propagated the legacy of a massive wisdom failure. Ultimately, the performance that counted for Solomon was his last one. One writer observed, "Solomon's kingdom was an outstanding example of wealth, military power, and prestige. Yet the true security of Israel did not rest in any of those things. It rested in the blessing of God and in the obedience and faithfulness of their king."[8]

in me. And the life I now live in the flesh I live by faith in the Son of God, who loved me and gave himself for me." This is a reality that Solomon did not know but one that can be the grace and guidepost of our pursuit of wisdom.

So coming full circle, let's return to Solomon's moment of choice, when God offered to grant the deepest wishes of his heart. Let's reconsider the possible answers we might give to such a proposal. Then let's think about the impact of Christ's words when he pronounced a truth that pointed to all that is available in his gospel: "Something greater than Solomon is here" (Matthew 12:42).

Proverbs gives God's people principles for wisdom. Jesus is the personification of that wisdom. Proverbs is wisdom in literature. Jesus is wisdom in life. He is the fulfillment of all Old Testament wisdom. So choose Christ! Follow Christ! Seek Christ! Abide in Christ! Cry out daily, even moment by moment, for his wisdom to empower you, change you, and guide you into a life of practical and lasting satisfaction.

There is a scene in the movie *Indiana Jones and the Last Crusade* that shows Indiana in pursuit of the Holy Grail (the cup Jesus used in the Last Supper). As Indiana enters the cave where he expects to make the discovery, he finds the treasure of a wide variety of cups guarded by a knight who has stayed alive (barely) for seven hundred years to protect the grail. At this moment, the bad guy and his female accomplice bust in. Knowing he too is in search of the grail, the knight announces to the couple, "You must choose. But choose wisely. For as the true grail will bring you life, the false grail will take it from you." The girl picks a beautiful gold cup from the vast selection. The bad guy proclaims, "This is a cup for the King of Kings. Eternal life!" He dips it in water and drinks. Suddenly he morphs into a skeleton and evaporates into dust. The knight guarding the cup says rather stoically, "He chose poorly." Now it is Indiana's turn. He finds a simple cup he describes as the "cup of a carpenter" and drinks. The knight announces, "You have chosen wisely."[10]

The wisdom of the world glistens like cheap glitter with false appeal and the phony promise of an accomplished life. Yet its waters produce disorder and worthless results. The wisdom of Christ—unassuming but proven, simple but supernatural, humble but holy—offers the promise of life. We cannot afford to choose poorly. May this book offer you the reassurance from above, and from those who watch your life, that you have chosen wisely.

Ready to Receive

Next time you read through the book of Proverbs, try to read and apply the book through a gospel lens. Think of every reference to wisdom as a promise fulfilled in the life of Christ. Let your heart resonate with thanks for the sufficiency of Jesus in providing all the wisdom you need for life and godliness.

As you remember the heartbreaking legacy of Solomon, consciously look to Jesus in wholehearted reliance. Think often of how he can empower you to apply wisdom to your relationships:

- with your spouse (if married) for the sake of a pure testimony,
- with your children for the sake of godly legacy,
- with your friends and associates for an exemplary testimony,
- and to your perseverance in the faith for the sake of a strong finish and a Christ-honoring eternal reward.

Take time to experience the following Wisdom Prayer, allowing the biblical truths to renew your mind as your prayerful response draws your heart closer to Christ, who is your wisdom.

Wisdom Prayers

Wisdom Sufficient for Your Life

Please see appendix 1 for an explanation of this New Testament approach to prayer. You are encouraged to set aside quality time to enjoy the prayer experiences as you finish each chapter. If you are studying this book with someone else, let these guides encourage your united prayers. The prompts provided are designed to help you pray from God's Word with helpful specificity and application but are not meant to restrict your prayers. Trust the Holy Spirit to guide your thoughts and words according to the biblical passages provided here.

As mentioned earlier, in spite of Solomon's sad ending, God inspired him to write much about wisdom in the books of Proverbs, Song of Solomon, probably Ecclesiastes, and even two psalms (72 and 127). Looking at Proverbs 3:1–8, we want to pray about how the God of wisdom, personified in Jesus Christ, is sufficient for our lives.

Proverbs 3:1–8

1 My son, do not forget my teaching, but let your heart keep my com-
mandments, 2 for length of days and years of life and peace they will
add to you. 3 Let not steadfast love and faithfulness forsake you; bind
them around your neck; write them on the tablet of your heart. 4 So
you will find favor and good success in the sight of God and man. 5
Trust in the Lord with all your heart, and do not lean on your own
understanding. 6 In all your ways acknowledge him, and he will make
straight your paths. 7 Be not wise in your own eyes; fear the Lord, and
turn away from evil. 8 It will be healing to your flesh and refreshment
to your bones.

REVERENCE—"Who is God?"

Lord Jesus, I worship you because you are:

- Truth (v. 1)
- The giver of life (v. 2)
- The God of peace (v. 2)
- The God of steadfast love (v. 3)
- Faithful (v. 3)

- The God who changes my heart (v. 3)
- The God of favor and blessing (v. 4)
- The God who sees all (v. 4)
- Trustworthy (v. 5)
- Worthy of my whole heart (v. 5)
- The God of perfect understanding (v. 5)
- Worthy of my all (v. 6)
- The One who directs my path (v. 6)
- All-wise (v. 7)
- Worthy to be feared (v. 7)
- Holy (v. 7)
- My healer (v. 8)
- My refresher (v. 8)

Thank you that your Word brought me peace (v. 2) when ______________________________.

Thank you that because of your steadfast love and faithfulness (v. 3), you did not forsake me when ______________________________.

Thank you that you have given me favor and blessing in my ______________________________. (v. 4)

RESPONSE—"How should I respond?"

I confess that instead of trusting you with my whole heart (v. 5), I often trust in ____________________ instead.

REQUESTS—"What should I pray about?"

Lord, give me grace to acknowledge you today when ______________________________. (v. 5)

Lord, please make the path straight for ____________________ [name] as they trust you for ______________________________. (v. 5)

READINESS—"Where am I headed?"

Help me to reject human wisdom and to fear you when I encounter the evil of ________________________. (v. 7)

REVERENCE—"Who is God?"

Thank you that you can bring healing and strength to my life today (v. 8) because you are ____.
[Draw from all the truths about his character noted above.]

2

Accessing Your Wisdom Treasure

> We are lost: but in the gospel thou hast presented to us a full, free and eternal salvation;
> Weak: but here we learn that help is found in One who is mighty,
> Poor: but in him we discover unsearchable riches,
> Blind: but we find he has treasures of wisdom and knowledge.
> We thank thee for thy unspeakable gift.
> Thy Son is our only refuge, foundation, hope, confidence. . . .
> May his glory fill our minds, his love reign in our affections, his cross inflame us with ardor. . . .
> And may every place and company we are in be benefited by us.[1]
>
> A Puritan Prayer

> The treasures of wisdom are hidden not from us, but for us, in Christ.
>
> Matthew Henry

The lines of aspiring customers were out the door at many gas stations, grocery stores, and other outlets. A last-minute frenzy swept the country in early 2016 as the unlikely, the unlucky, and the typically uninterested public purchased their tickets for a chance to win the all-time-high Powerball jackpot of $1.5 billion. Leading into the drawing, there had been nineteen consecutive Powerball drawings with no winner. Just two weeks prior, the grand prize had been a cool $400 million.

After the winning numbers were revealed, the largest lottery prize in history was split three ways. Statisticians had figured the odds of winning the jackpot were 1 in 292 million. Still, millions took the risk. One guy I spoke to said, "Hey, if I don't buy a ticket I can't win. It's worth a shot."

When it comes to the priceless treasure of transformational wisdom, you have more than a shot. You have a promise. In fact, you have an abundance of reassurances that your odds are one-in-one *if* you know Christ and are willing to call on him. There is no gamble, only a guarantee. He is the one in whom all the treasures of wisdom and knowledge are available. You might say he purchased the "winning ticket" on your behalf through the sacrifice of his life on the cross.

In part 2, we are going to look at the life qualities God is eager to produce in you and through your relationships with others. But first, I want to inspire you to pray with genuine expectation and a firm biblical assurance about God's desire to answer the prayer for wisdom.

Assurances of Wisdom

Solomon punctuated the book of Proverbs with assurances that underscore God's desire to impart wisdom:

- "Let the wise hear and increase in learning" (1:5)
- "Wisdom cries aloud in the street, in the markets she raises her voice" (1:20)
- "[Make] your ear attentive to wisdom" (2:2)
- "Seek it like silver and search for it as for hidden treasures" (2:4)
- "The Lord gives wisdom" and "stores up sound wisdom for the upright" (2:6–7)
- "Get wisdom!" (4:5, 7)

Wisdom Better Than Solomon

So why do I share Solomon's story on the front end of a book that is supposed to be about a gospel-empowered wisdom? Primarily, to affirm that God loves to answer our cry for wisdom. At the same time, the roller coaster experiences of the wisest man in Old Testament history leaves us conflicted. Clearly we all have a compelling and continual need for God's wisdom even as Solomon sought it and, in so many ways, demonstrated it. Yet, like Solomon, we recognize that our human capacity for the faithful application and stewardship of that wisdom is flawed and fickle.

Any pursuit of wisdom must include the weighty summary Solomon expressed at the conclusion of Ecclesiastes: "The end of the matter; all has been heard. Fear God and keep his commandments, for this is the whole duty of man. For God will bring every deed into judgment, with every secret thing, whether good or evil" (Ecclesiastes 12:13–14). In many ways, and in spite of his colossal personal failures, Solomon came full circle.

"Fear God." These had been Solomon's inspired and repeated words in Proverbs. "The fear of the Lord is the beginning of wisdom, and the knowledge of the Holy One is insight" (Proverbs 9:10, and reiterated in 1:7, 29; 2:5; 3:7; 8:13; 14:2, 6, 26–27; 15:33; and 16:16). As far back as the earliest recorded book of the Bible, this truth rang out: "Behold, the fear of the Lord, that is wisdom, and to turn away from evil is understanding" (Job 28:28). Over three hundred times the Bible refers to the idea of fear in connection to God.

So to avoid the confusion and counterfeits that seek to draw us away from true wisdom, we must resolutely fear God. How? To fear God means to know him, revere him, obey him, and trust him. As one writer described it, "The fear of the Lord is a state of mind in which one's own attitudes, will, feelings, deeds, and goals are exchanged for God's."[9]

From a New Testament standpoint, what would it mean to "fear" God with the commitment to know him, to trust and obey him, to exchange all that you are for all that he is? Very simply, this is the life of Christ, living in us. As Paul declared in Galatians 2:20, "I have been crucified with Christ. It is no longer I who live, but Christ who lives

I could go on citing dozens of other examples. But in summary, Solomon offers thirty-one chapters that extol the benefits of a wise life, underscored by God's eagerness to give it to us.

God's Generous Promise

The New Testament book of James is written to Christians who are scattered, struggling, and in need of God's sufficiency—much like many of us. In the first chapter, James pronounces a supreme truth that inspires confident prayer: "If any of you lacks wisdom, let him ask God, who gives generously to all without reproach, and it will be given him" (James 1:5).

News Flash: Any Christian can call out to God for wisdom. We do not need a human intermediary. We do not have to go through a priest, a pastor, or a theologian. Just ask—directly, openly, and earnestly. We simply must sense and admit our need for wisdom beyond our own resources and abilities. The longer I live, the easier that is. My "ask" seems more frequent these days, not just because of my sense of need but because of my deepening awareness of God's readiness to give it.

The directive to "ask" is not just a suggestion. This is what is called an imperative verb in the Greek language. God is not giving pleasant advice. He is commanding his children to ask. As pastor John MacArthur describes it, "Although God has wisdom in abundance and is infinitely more willing to impart his wisdom than we are to ask for it, he nevertheless expects us to ask him for it."[2] The command is forceful here because God, as the all-knowing, all-good Creator, sees what we need during challenging times. We might feel tempted instead to talk to a friend, read a book, or sign up for a seminar. These could be helpful, but one thing we *must* do is to ask God for his wisdom in the perplexing and painful situations of life. Some people try to cope or escape through entertainment, hobbies, or addictive stimulants. All of these are cheap and unnecessary substitutes for God's wisdom.

God's Generous Character

Our confidence in this prayer is not about the fancy words we use, the spiritual mood we are sensing, or even the earnestness of our need.

Our faith is centered in the character of God. He is all-wise and the only true source of wisdom (Romans 11:33–36; 16:27). He is a God who "gives generously without reproach." It's just who he is.

James' understanding of God giving generously is literally the idea of "one who gives sincerely, without hesitation or mental reservation. He does not grumble or criticize. His commitment to his people is total and unreserved: they can expect to receive."[3]

In his own teaching on prayer, Jesus instructed his disciples to "ask" of God continuously (Matthew 6:6; Luke 11:9). He followed with this heavy-duty assurance: "If you then, who are evil, know how to give good gifts to your children, how much more will the heavenly Father give the Holy Spirit to those who ask him!" (Luke 11:13, also Matthew 6:11). Our completely good and wise Father, through the work of his Son, gives us the wisdom that is abundantly ours by his presence in our lives through the Holy Spirit, the "Spirit of Wisdom" (Isaiah 11:2; Ephesians 1:17).

Waiting for Us to Ask

And just to underscore this incredible assurance, the Bible says God gives "without reproach." To reproach means "to upbraid, to severely reprimand." If a child were to ask a parent for a shovel to whack the family dog over the head, the response would naturally be "What's wrong with you? Why would you even ask for that?" God, on the other hand, responds to our need for wisdom with "I was waiting for you to ask! Here you go."

One commentator writes, "The believer should have no hesitation in asking God for wisdom as if God would scold us for not already having all the wisdom we need."[4] John Calvin affirmed, "Since we see that the Lord does not so require from us what is above our strength, but that he is ready to help us, provided we ask, let us, therefore, learn, whenever he commands anything, to ask of him the power to perform it."[5] God's very character is such that he loves to answer our prayer for wisdom.

Just a reminder, the nature of this wisdom-gift from God brings great assurance. Commenting on the biblical times' understanding of wisdom, Canadian theologian Peter Davids states, "Wisdom would make or keep him (the pray-er) perfect or enable him to stand. Similarly, in the New Testament wisdom is closely associated with understanding the divine plan and responding to it."[6] This wisdom brings alignment with God's purposes, strength, endurance, perspective, and empowerment to do God's will. As we will see in the part 2, this ignites a lifestyle of godly character and Christ-honoring relationships.

Wisdom Glorifies Jesus

One final reason God loves to answer your prayer for wisdom is that gospel wisdom glorifies Jesus. Why? Let's remind ourselves of what the New Testament tells us about the wisdom of Jesus:

- Christ's wisdom is greater than all of Solomon's wisdom. (Luke 11:31)
- Christ himself and the preaching of his gospel is the supreme wisdom of God. (1 Corinthians 1:20–25)
- Christ is the source of our very life and IS our wisdom so that all our boasting will be in him. (1 Corinthians 1:30–31)
- God wants to lavish upon us "all wisdom and insight," that we would know his will and fulfill his purposes. (Ephesians 1:8)
- God wants to give us the "Spirit of wisdom and of revelation" that we might know him, the hope of his calling, and his power within us. (Ephesians 1:17–19)
- God wants us to be "filled . . . with all spiritual wisdom and understanding" so that we will live "in a manner worthy of the Lord." (Colossians 1:9–10)
- And again, Christ is the one in whom are hidden all the treasures of wisdom and knowledge. (Colossians 2:3)

So we can pray for this incredible wisdom with the confidence that Christ will be glorified in us and through us. He is honored when his wisdom becomes more and more real in our daily lives, homes, workplaces, churches, and communities.

The Potential for Christ-Glorifying Wisdom

I love the prophetic description in the book of Isaiah about the life and power of the coming Messiah: "And the Spirit of the Lord shall rest upon him, the Spirit of wisdom and understanding, the Spirit of counsel and might, the Spirit of knowledge and the fear of the Lord" (Isaiah 11:2). Fast-forwarding to the final hours Jesus spent with his disciples, as his earthly ministry was culminating and he faced the cross, we find Jesus offering this amazing promise: "Truly, truly, I say to you, whoever believes in me will also do the works that I do; and greater works than these will he do because I am going to the Father" (John 14:12). Specifically, Jesus is referring to their fulfillment of his great gospel Commission (Matthew 28:18–20) through the power of the indwelling Holy Spirit. His earthly ministry had been primarily limited to his physical presence. Now that presence would be dispersed in supernatural influence through the lives of all those who would believe in him.

Today we can and must exhibit this "Spirit of wisdom and understanding" that so evidently rested on Christ's earthly mission. The potential of his wise and understanding life in us and through us to minister and relate to others is truly staggering.

The Promise for Christ-Glorifying Wisdom

Note what Jesus says next in this Upper Room address: "Whatever you ask in my name, this I will do, that the Father may be glorified in the Son. If you ask me anything in my name, I will do it" (John 14:13–14). In this statement, he was not instructing us to add a sacred three-word addendum to our sometimes scattered and misaligned prayers. Rather, he is saying, "When you pray the way you know I would pray—I will do it." Or, said another way, "When you pray consistent with my character and mission—I will do it." His purpose, stated clearly here, in all of our praying, is that "the Father may be glorified in the Son."

I would suggest that an earnest request for "wisdom from above" not only reflects the life and character of Jesus, but it is a prayer whose answer brings glory to God.

The Provision of Christ-Glorifying Wisdom

Let's stay with our all-wise savior for just another moment in this Upper Room interchange. Next, Jesus says, "If you love me, you will keep my commandments. And I will ask the Father, and he will give you another helper, to be with you forever, even the Spirit of truth, whom the world cannot receive, because it neither sees him nor knows him. You know him, for he dwells with you and will be in you. I will not leave you as orphans; I will come to you" (John 14:15–18).

Yes, we love Jesus. We want to keep his commandments. One of those commandments, and the most immediate in this context, is to pray in his name for the glory of the Father. As we pray this way, it is inspiring to remember that the same Spirit that rested upon and was powerfully evident throughout Jesus' ministry lives in us. Now, through his finished work on the cross, that Spirit is in residence and is revealed in the lives of his followers. If this were not true, we would be like orphans—abandoned, alone, and without the necessary resources for a rewarding life.

Just for our encouragement, let's take a quick look at the other realities he described in his message to his disciples concerning his future presence in them:

> But when the helper comes, whom I will send to you from the Father, the Spirit of truth, who proceeds from the Father, he will bear witness about me. And you also will bear witness, because you have been with me from the beginning.
>
> John 15:26–27

This blessed assurance continues. As you read, keep in mind your need for daily wisdom.

> When the Spirit of truth comes, he will guide you into all the truth, for he will not speak on his own authority, but whatever he hears he will speak, and he will declare to you the things that are to come. He will glorify me, for he will take what is mine and declare it to you. All that the Father has is mine; therefore I said that he will take what is mine and declare it to you.
>
> John 16:13–15

All that is the Father's is Christ's. All that is Christ's is taught by the Spirit. All that is the Spirit's is in us for the glory of Jesus. Like a golden thread woven through a royal garment, this formula radiates with the promise of wisdom.

Access! Abide! Ask!

Not long ago, a friend invited our family to attend a presidential primary debate. We were excited to have this first-time experience that turned out to be quite animated and inspiring. But there was no way we were going to get into that highly secured environment without an access pass that had been provided by a credible and connected friend. Jesus is our access pass to the treasures of limitless wisdom, found in him and experienced by his Spirit and his Word.

Now we have the privilege and responsibility of enjoying this access to the fullest as we walk with him. One more peek into the Upper Room reminds us of the core message he gave to his disciples and to us:

> Abide in me, and I in you. As the branch cannot bear fruit by itself, unless it abides in the vine, neither can you, unless you abide in me. I am the vine; you are the branches. Whoever abides in me and I in him, he it is that bears much fruit, for apart from me you can do nothing.
>
> John 15:4–5

To abide means to "stay connected" and to "derive our life" from the source—which is Jesus. Supernatural wisdom flows from his life to ours because his life is in ours. In truth, his life is our life.

The fullness of the triune God is committed to our growth in Christlike wisdom. One writer puts it this way:

- *The Father* wants us to bear the image in which he first created us.
- *The Son* sets before us the perfect image to which we are to be confirmed.
- *The Spirit* works in us to transform us into the image of Christ.[7]

Now we must ask—faithfully, consistently, enduringly. Wisdom is assured by God. Wisdom is the expression of his generous character. Wisdom palpably glorifies Jesus. James' words hold fresh promise now: "If any of you lacks wisdom, let him ask God, who gives generously to all without reproach, and it will be given him" (James 1:5).

It's been said that nothing is dynamic until it is specific. Specificity fuels authenticity. In the pages ahead I hope you will discover the power of wisdom unleashed in day-to-day life as you get specific and unpack wisdom from above using God's definition—and trusting in his lavish provision.

Ready to Receive

With the promise of wisdom given in James 1:5, try to renew your mind each day in the truth of the astounding and unfathomable generosity of God's character. Fix your faith in the truth of his limitless supply and willing heart as a motivation to ask with vigorous belief and boldness.

Every time you ask for wisdom, assess your motivation. Remember the great Westminster Catechism that declares, "The chief end of man is to glorify God and enjoy Him forever." Set your heart on asking for wisdom so that God will be glorified and Christ will be enjoyed with every fiber of your being.

Take time to experience the following Wisdom Prayer, allowing the biblical truths to renew your mind as your prayerful response draws your heart closer to Christ, who is your wisdom.

Wisdom Prayer

God's Treasure, Your Transformation

At the end of the eleventh chapter of Romans, Paul gives a powerful benediction based on the gospel doctrine he taught in the previous chapters. He then makes an appeal for a worship-driven response starting in chapter 12. We will pray from these two dynamically connected passages.

Romans 11:33–12:2

33 Oh, the depth of the riches and wisdom and knowledge of God! How
unsearchable are his judgments and how inscrutable his ways! 34 "For
who has known the mind of the Lord, or who has been his counselor?"
35 "Or who has given a gift to him that he might be repaid?" 36 For from
him and through him and to him are all things. To him be glory forever.
Amen. 1 I appeal to you therefore, brothers, by the mercies of God, to
present your bodies as a living sacrifice, holy and acceptable to God,
which is your spiritual worship. 2 Do not be conformed to this world, but
be transformed by the renewal of your mind, that by testing you may
discern what is the will of God, what is good and acceptable and perfect.

REVERENCE—"Who is God?"

Lord, I worship you because you are . . .

- Rich in wisdom (v. 33)
- Rich in knowledge (v. 33)
- The God of unsearchable judgments (v. 33)
- The God whose ways are beyond understanding (v. 34)
- Self-sufficient (v. 35)
- The source, the means, and the end of all things (v. 36)
- Worthy of eternal glory (v. 36)
- Merciful (v. 1)
- Worthy of my complete sacrifice (v. 1)
- Worthy of my worship (v. 1)

- Able to transform my mind and life (v. 1)
- A revealer of your will (v. 2)
- Working in me that which is good, acceptable, and perfect in your sight (v. 2)

I praise you, Lord, that the riches of your wisdom and knowledge are more valuable than ______________________________. (v. 33)

I praise you that you are the source, the means and the end of ______________________ [specific elements of this life]. (v. 36)

RESPONSE—"How should I respond?"

Because you are worthy of eternal glory (v. 36), I also want to glorify you on this earth by ______________________________________.

Because of your mercy, I present ___________________________ [areas of your life] to you in complete surrender as my acceptable worship. (v. 1)

REQUESTS—"What should I pray about?"

Renew my mind so that I will not be conformed to the world when ______________________________. (v. 2)

Renew and transform _____________________________, that he/she will not be conformed to the world. (v. 2)

READINESS—"Where am I headed?"

When I am confronted with ______________________________ [an issue/struggle/relationships], help me to test it so that I might discern your will. (v. 2)

REVERENCE—"Who is God?"

Thank you that because your will is good, acceptable, and perfect, it is more satisfying to me than ____________________________________. (v. 2)

3

The Relational Game Changer

> Relationships are the atmosphere we need in order to survive. Infants who are not held fail to thrive, life-long partners die within months of each other, and loneliness is the greatest cause of suicide. The religion of Jesus was relationship, not rules, because that is what we need to survive.[1]
>
> Mark Baker, PhD

> As Christians we should be studying and modeling our lives and the life of the church on Jesus' relationships—with the Father and the Holy Spirit within the Trinity; with his followers, disciples and friends; with the crowds, the poor, the marginalized and the disabled; with men, women and children; with his opponents and enemies, politicians and religious leaders; with his own fellow Jews, Samaritans and Gentiles. . . . Jesus' relationships are an essential element in his calling. This was to reveal the nature of God and to be the model for the life of the church as a body and for each one of us individually as his followers.[2]
>
> Martin Goldsmith

Before we jump into the next section, which portrays the practical elements of a wise gospel lifestyle, let's talk about some things that are at the core of your soul. After all, the subtitle of this book makes a bold promise—that Christ's wisdom can address your greatest needs.

We've all known highly successful and quite impressive people who have excelled in their professional pursuits but failed miserably in relationships. Without using names to expose the guilty, I think of:

- A wealthy businessman who knew how to run a company and found great financial success but destroyed his marriage and was despised by his children.
- A lifelong pastor, skilled preacher, and astute theologian who dishonored his wife and alienated his children.
- A community-activist mom who helped organize school programs, drove her children to excel, and was a go-to person for projects in the church but cheated on her husband.

I am guessing you have known these people too, plus a dozen more just like them. Although the names and locations vary, the behaviors are all too common.

Were these people wise? Well, yes—and no. They utilized knowledge and skill in order to accomplish something. This would demonstrate some of the qualities we often recognize as practical acumen and even found—to some degree—in the book of Proverbs. However, from a New Testament standpoint, these high-achievers were fools. Foolish people annihilate relationships on the altar of accomplishment.

An annual survey revealed recently that nearly 41 percent of Americans said they didn't take a single vacation day during the previous calendar year, almost exactly the same number as the year before that. According to the survey, almost 17 percent said they took fewer than five vacation days.[3] Whatever this reveals about us, it is clear that many of us are so obsessed with the idea of "human doings" that we may have forgotten how to be "human beings." As a mentor of mine used to say, "Busyness destroys relationships."

Your Paramount Needs

So as we jump all in with the importance of wisdom in life, let me ask, "What are your greatest needs in this earthly journey?"

As a pastor for over thirty years, I have encountered sincere believers who have not given a lot of thought to this query. I've also known many whose answers were superficial and unsatisfying.

Distinguished author and rabbi Harold Kushner wrote, "No one ever said on their deathbed, 'I wish I'd spent more time at the office.'" The notoriety of this statement stirs something within us.

Let's be honest. No mother comes to the end of her life wishing she had watched one more series on HGTV. She does long for her children to be assured of her abiding love. No businessman desires to have his portfolios neatly stacked next to his deathbed as he takes his final breath. He does desire to be surrounded by caring, grateful family and friends. No doctor takes her last breath obsessed with disappointment that she did not write just one more article for that medical journal. Rather, she longs to remember the faces of patients whose lives were changed by her attentive care. No Christian steps across the threshold to eternity regretful that he did not sign another petition protesting a liberal government. He does rejoice in the lives that came to Christ and will join him in heaven because of his personal influence for the gospel.

So I ask again, "What are your greatest, most profound needs in this earthly journey?" Instinctively we know that there is something beyond the noise of a society that allures us to pursue temporary notoriety, artificial accomplishments, shallow social-media connections, and the accumulation of more stuff.

Note: Our Creator's supreme commands for our lives are simple, pure, and pointed. They resound unmistakably: Love God, love others (Matthew 22:37–40). These are the highest and best prescriptions of the power of the gospel. We now can have transforming love relationships with a holy God. We now have supernatural capacity to experience this love in community: the community of marriage, family, friendship, and Christian fellowship. Because he knows our core longings and he desires our highest good, he calls us to pursue loving, meaningful relationships with all our heart, soul, mind, and strength.

So I propose that your deepest needs are relational. When we reflect on the purpose of life, we are not compelled toward a greater sense of professional accomplishment but awakened to meaningful satisfaction with authentic relationships.

That is where wisdom intersects our path with supernatural force. New Testament wisdom is more than a set of pithy sayings to help us climb just a little higher on the ladder of secular achievement. I say it again, **New Testament wisdom = Jesus Christ—embraced, experienced, exemplified, and exalted in our lives and relationships.**

Wisdom = Authentic Relationships

In the process of praying through the concepts of this book, reading prolifically, and preparing to write, I have been struck with an amazing truth, like a lightning burst of insight in the dimness of a summer evening in Colorado. Here it is: New Testament wisdom always excels in authentic relationships. You could say that the acid test of real gospel wisdom is the quality and godliness of interpersonal relationships.

In fact, I am astounded by the parallels between four of the great "lists" of gospel behavior. These passages are all familiar and famous to most, but each is primarily relational and they all have similarities. They are:

- The Beatitudes (Matthew 5:2–12)
- The Marks of Genuine Love (1 Corinthians 13:4–8)
- The Fruit of the Spirit (Galatians 5:22–23)
- The Wisdom from Above (James 3:17–18)

(For a summary of the parallels, see the chart in appendix 2.)

In the pages ahead, I believe what you read will bring life-changing empowerment to your marriage, your parenting, your friendships, your work interactions, your interface with nonbelievers, and the future trajectory of your life.

In all probability, your traditional understanding of wisdom might be assisting you in spending more successful and productive time at the office—or other tasks of choice. What we will discover in the following chapters will provide insight and assurance that will eventually bring you to the final chapter of your life with a higher accomplishment—relationships that honored Christ and made the journey truly rewarding.

Gospel wisdom is not just about making good decisions concerning a future course. It is more about making the best decisions on how to love your wife, respect your husband, nurture your children, and honor your parents. New Testament wisdom is not just about finding the right strategy to achieve a profitable outcome. Rather, it is about finding the best way to reflect Christ's character as you esteem your friends, serve your neighbors, pray for your church leaders, and inspire your work associates with the example of a godly and relational life. Why do I propose this? Let's visit some islands of New Testament truth and see.

The "Logos" of God's Love

The apostle John helps us understand God's plan for revealing his wisdom to us in Christ, even before creation, and in our lives today. This account of the gospel starts off:

> In the beginning was the Word, and the Word was with God, and the Word was God. He was in the beginning with God. All things were made through him, and without him was not anything made that was made. In him was life, and the life was the light of men.
>
> John 1:1–4

The eternal Word who created the world and came as Savior is identified here with the Greek term *logos*. Many insightful and quite complicated theories exist concerning the background of this word and John's choice of it. However, experts agree that in essence, this word demonstrates that Christ is the personification and ultimate representation of the character and wisdom of God.

Not only did Christ preexist the creation of this world (as God), but John also says "the Word was *with* God." That is not just the idea of hanging out passively in the same celestial space. It means "perfect fellowship . . . equality and intimacy, face to face with each other."[4] So this ultimate divine wisdom personified in Christ did not just exist in a vacuum but in a perfect coequal, loving, harmonious relationship with the Father. As one writer explained,

> If it was this *same* Word, and no other, who was himself God, and who, from all eternity, was in active communion with God, then the statement follows naturally that all things were created through him, thus bringing the essential nature of the Word and his manifestation in creation into connection. As the idea of the Word involves knowledge and will, wisdom, and force, the creative function is properly his. Hence his close relation to created things, especially to man, prepares the way for his incarnation and redeeming work.[5]

Interpretation: Christ revealed his perfect, divine, eternal, and relational wisdom by demonstrating his love for sinful mankind in order to bring them back to himself in saving, transforming relationship.

Throughout John's account of Christ, whose "life was the light of men," we see our Lord reconciling to himself those lost in the darkness of sin. No better summary exists concerning the purpose of Christ as the personification of God's wisdom than this: "For God so loved the world, that he gave his only Son, that whoever believes in him should not perish but have eternal life" (John 3:16).

Relational Teacher

Our all-wise Jesus demonstrated the ultimate impact of biblical wisdom in the quality of his relationships. We see it throughout his ministry in caring for the outcast, the diseased, the bereaved, the disregarded, the broken, the ignorant, and the lost. Volumes have been written about the model of his life.

Of course, the bulk of his relational efforts were invested in his closest disciples. John 13:1 introduces the scene of Jesus as he gathers one final time with his disciples to celebrate the Passover, using this descriptor, "Jesus knew that his hour had come to depart out of this world to the Father, having loved his own who were in the world, he loved them to the end." The literal meaning indicates that he loved them "to the uttermost," or to the ultimate limits of love. This commitment was reflected in his heartfelt words to them as they gathered, "This is my commandment, that you love one another as I have loved you. Greater love has no one than this, that someone lay down his life for his friends" (John 15:12–13). They were to respond by loving one another after his example. They would also eventually give their very lives for him and his life-changing gospel message, but not before they had turned the world upside down (Acts 17:6) with the wisdom of his gospel of love and truth.

The Corinthian Call

The application of Jesus' wisdom to relationships also resonates in the letters of the apostle Paul. In 1 Corinthians, the Holy Spirit inspired Paul to spend extensive amounts of effort describing the difference between the superficiality and insufficiency of the wisdom of the world in contrast to the wisdom that comes through Christ and the message of his cross. The theme of wisdom (both worldly and divine) is mentioned in the first two chapters no fewer than nineteen times.

But what prompted this flurry of wisdom-oriented teaching? What was Paul's concern? Put simply, he was addressing a relationally broken church that was manifesting the negative effects that occur when believers operated on anything other than gospel wisdom.

The springboard into his wisdom mini-sermon was this concern: "I appeal to you, brothers, by the name of our Lord Jesus Christ, that all of you agree, and that there be no divisions among you, but that you be united in the same mind and the same judgment" (1 Corinthians 1:10). At the end of his wisdom descriptions, he again reiterates, "But I, brothers, could not address you as spiritual people, but as people of the flesh, as infants in Christ. . . . For while there is jealousy and strife among you, are you not of the flesh and behaving only in a human way?" (1 Corinthians 3:1, 3).

The context of Paul presenting Christ as our wisdom was to correct relational breakdown that had resulted from a reliance on the world's way to thinking and relating. New Testament wisdom, if it has any application at all (which it does in paramount ways), must have ultimate relevance to how we relate to one another.

The Colossian Connection

Another landmark declaration of Christ as the essence of wisdom is found in Colossians. Again, Christ is the One in whom are hidden all the treasures of wisdom and knowledge (Colossians 2:3). Based on this reality, Paul prayed that the believers in Colosse would be "filled with the knowledge of his will in all spiritual wisdom and understanding" (1:9). Why did he pray this? The text explains, "So as to walk in a manner worthy of the Lord, fully pleasing to him, bearing fruit in every good work and increasing in the knowledge of God" (1:10).

What was the goal of this spiritual wisdom? The knowledge of more theological facts? Information for creating better Bible maps? Moral principles for getting ahead in life? No, those are good things, but the goal was a deeper *relationship* with the Lord that produced the fruit of an authentic, abiding life. As the theologian J. I. Packer explained, "The kind of wisdom that God waits to give to those who ask him, is a wisdom that will bind us to himself, a wisdom that will find expression in a spirit of faith and life of faithfulness."[6] The first goal of New Testament wisdom is that we would know Christ.

In the next chapter, Paul continues in his struggle on behalf of the Colossians as he prays for them (2:1). His goal in this exhortation is that "their hearts may be encouraged, being knit together in love" (2:2). Again, his prayer is prompted by a relational concern for these believers—mutual encouragement and a loving, close connection to one another in Christ. This concern was rooted in strong assurance that they would "reach all the riches of full assurance of understanding and the knowledge of God's mystery, which is Christ, in whom are hidden all the treasures of wisdom and knowledge" (2:2–3).

To make the point again, this focus on the sufficient wisdom of Christ would ultimately be applied—not to some church-building program, the solving of a complex budget issue, or the charting of new ministry strategy—but in vital and growing relationship with Christ and one another as they encountered the onslaught of the false wisdom of their day.

A Brother's Concern

We will spend the bulk of this book talking about the qualities of Christ seen in James' description of the "wisdom from above" in James 3:17–18. But in quick summary, we should note that James (the half brother of Christ) had a primary concern for the relationship struggles that existed among the believers to whom he wrote. Specifically he confronted them about:

- Anger (1:19–20)
- Prejudice and partiality (2:2–13)
- A lack of compassion for the needy (1:27; 2:14–17; 5:1–6)
- Unbridled tongues and relationally destructive speech (1:26; 3:1–12; 4:11–12)
- Jealousy, selfish ambition, and relational disorder (3:14–16)
- Interpersonal quarrels and fights (4:1–2)

What did they require in order to remedy these relational woes? Not another self-help book about better communication. Not more savvy negotiation skills. Not a seminar on anger management. They needed "wisdom from above" (3:17–18) and were compelled to ask God for this wisdom with the assurance that he was generous in giving it to them (1:5).

Again, the New Testament understanding of wisdom is all about genuine, transformed, Christ-honoring relationships. If we think we are wise but our relationships are not authentic and Christ-worthy, then we have misunderstood the wisdom that is available and expected in the message of the gospel.

Misrepresenting the Mission

More is on the line than simply our ability to hold hands, get along, and sing songs about the love of God. As representatives of Christ we are on mission. We are the expression of his life on this earth. The local church is the agency for proclaiming this relationally powerful wisdom of the gospel.

In his classic book *The Mark of the Christian*, the late Francis Schaeffer reminded us of the relational core of our mission as he quoted these words of Jesus: "A new commandment I give to you, that you love one another: just as I have loved you, you also are to love one another. By this all people will know that you are my disciples, if you have love for one another" (John 13:34–35).

Schaeffer convincingly points out, "This passage reveals the mark that Jesus gives to label a Christian not just in one era or in one locality but at all times and in all places until Jesus returns."[7] He drills the point home noting,

> Upon his authority Jesus gives the world the right to judge whether you and I are born-again Christians on the basis of our observable love toward all Christians. . . . if people come up to us and cast in our teeth the judgment that we are not a Christian because we have not shown love toward other Christians, we must understand that they are only exercising a prerogative which Jesus gave them.[8]

Shaeffer goes on to advocate for true oneness, forgiveness, and a visible, costly commitment to one another, despite our differences. He also notes, "Without true Christians loving one another, Christ says the world cannot be expected to listen, even when we are giving proper answers."[9]

Proper answers. I guess that's what I thought wisdom was all about for most of my Christian life. Of course, proper answers matter, but they fall short of the real power of our impact on a rapidly disintegrating and skeptical culture. Answers authenticated by true love are the need of the hour. Relationships authenticated by gospel wisdom are absolutely critical. But how?

We must rediscover the power and promise of Christ's supernatural, self-sacrificing love. We must abide in him so that the true wisdom of his life emanates in all that we do and say—and in how we demonstrate his love to others. And now we must rediscover his eagerness to accomplish all of this, and more, on behalf of those who simply ask.

Ready to Receive

As you consider the relational implications of gospel wisdom, reflect on appendix 2. As you read down each vertical column from the various passages, make it your goal that in your prayers for wisdom you will keep these characteristics always in mind.

Now assess that same chart again. With a careful and unrushed spirit, work your way down each of the vertical columns again with this simple prayer: "Lord Jesus, thank you that you are ________________ and that you have the power to make me like you."

In one more review of this chart, work your way down each vertical column, considering the character quality in each box. Ask the Lord to bring to mind the name of a specific person with this prayer: "Give me wisdom to show this expression of your life to ________________________ [name]."

Take time to experience the following Wisdom Prayer, allowing the biblical truths to renew your mind as your prayerful response draws your heart closer to Christ, who is your wisdom.

Wisdom Prayer

Jesus, the Great Relater

In the opening verses of John's wonderful gospel, we see both the relationship with Jesus in eternity with the Father prior to coming to earth and a summary of his relational strategy with those he came to save. We will use portions of this section as a basis of our praying.

John 1:1–5, 9–14

1 In the beginning was the Word, and the Word was with God, and the
Word was God. 2 He was in the beginning with God. 3 All things were
made through him, and without him was not any thing made that was
made. 4 In him was life, and the life was the light of men. 5 The light

shines in the darkness, and the darkness has not overcome it. . . . [9] The
true light, which gives light to everyone, was coming into the world. [10] He
was in the world, and the world was made through him, yet the world
did not know him. [11] He came to his own, and his own people did not
receive him. [12] But to all who did receive him, who believed in his name,
he gave the right to become children of God, [13] who were born, not of
blood nor of the will of the flesh nor of the will of man, but of God. [14]
And the Word became flesh and dwelt among us, and we have seen his
glory, glory as of the only Son from the Father, full of grace and truth.

REVERENCE—"Who is God?"

Lord Jesus, I worship you because you are . . .

- You are the Word—God's revelation of himself to man (v. 1)
- You existed in perfect intimacy with the Father in eternity past (v. 1)
- You are God (v. 1)
- You created all things (vv. 2–3)
- You are life (v. 4)
- Your life is the light of men (v. 4)
- You overcome darkness (v. 5)
- You make us children of God by receiving your life (v. 12)
- You have caused me to be born again by the power of God (v. 13)
- You dwelt among man in perfect relationship (v. 14)
- You are glorious (v. 14)
- You are the only Son from the Father (v.14)
- You are full of grace (v. 14)
- You are full of truth (v. 14)

I praise you, Lord Jesus, that you are the creator (vv. 2–3) of ________ ______________ [specific elements of creation].

I praise you that because you have given me life (v. 4), I ______________ [express the benefits of new life in him].

I praise you that your light overcame the darkness of my ______________________. (vv. 4–5)

RESPONSE—"How should I respond?"

I confess that there have been times when you came to me but in ignorance, I did not receive your ______________________. (v. 11)

REQUESTS—"What should I pray about?"

Because your life is my light, keep me from looking for light (direction, truth) in other places like ______________________. (v. 4)

I pray for ______________________, who does not know you and has not received you. May your light shine on them through me that they may be born of God. (vv. 12–13)

Because your relationships were marked by grace and truth (v. 14), help me today in my relationship with ______________________.
May I also manifest grace and truth when ______________________.

READINESS—"Where am I headed?"

As I head into a dark world, I trust your light to overcome ______________________ [specific temptations, attacks, conflicts]. (v. 5)

REVERENCE—"Who is God?"

I praise you that I can expect to see the fullness of your grace today when ______________________. (v. 14)

I praise you that I can trust in the fullness of your truth to produce ______________________. (v. 14)

PART TWO

Best Wisdom Practices

4

Purely Wise in a Wicked World

> But the wisdom from above is first pure.
>
> James 3:17

> The reason we are drawn to him is not because of his courage, his sympathy, his patience, or his brotherliness; it so because we feel instinctively that he is far above us, a man without a sin. It is this which gives the Christian church its power. The Christian church has but one perfect possession, that is Jesus.[1]
>
> Charles Edward Jefferson

Years ago, while working as associate pastor and personal assistant to Dr. John MacArthur, I was assigned to coordinate the yearly donor cruises sponsored by John's radio ministry, *Grace to You*. At one of the ports of call, I took advantage of an excursion to do some deep sea diving in the pristine waters of St. Thomas. Accompanied by a few buddies, we descended under the watchful eye of our instructor. Once I figured out the mechanics, I was arrested by the crystal clear luminosity of the blue Caribbean paradise. The brilliant colors of the tropical fish, the varieties of shells, and the clarity of it all left me in awe. It was like discovering a whole new world of dazzling brilliance with newly reborn eyes.

Contrast that amazement to a snorkeling attempt I pursued in high school in the lake where our family lived in southern New Mexico. The lake was fed by the muddy Rio Grande River. Swimming near the inlet, I made numerous attempts to see something other than my hand right in front of my face. Posthaste, I conceded the effort, realizing that the water was simply too dirty to enjoy any kind of aquatic sightseeing.

Just as navigating in a body of water is more enjoyable in pristine and unobstructed surroundings, so should it be with life. Yet this ideal has been lost in today's culture.

Selective Pursuits of Purity

In spite of the obvious moral decline of our society, we still love purity—at least selectively. We seem obsessed with pure water, evidenced by the incredible sales of bottled H_2O and in-home filtering systems. We know that impure water can result in intestinal sickness short-term and endangered health long-term.

The major nations of the world convene to address the dangers of polluted air. Contaminated food can tank a food-supply company or restaurant almost overnight when E. coli or other food-borne illnesses are discovered. Yes, we value purity when it comes to the health of our bodies.

But when it comes to the health of our souls and relationships, purity seems a passé and discarded commodity. Our culture has pursued values and behaviors that have polluted and corrupted our relationships. As a result, marriages, families, friendships, and churches have suffered.

Muddied Relationships

I think of another water encounter that occurred on a clear, sunny day when our family hiked near the base of Mount Rainier in Washington

State. An hour into our excursion, we discovered an alpine lake with a perfect view of the towering summit. The call of a cool swim on this warm August day was too compelling. Soon we shed our shoes and headed for the refreshment. The water was amazingly pure, allowing us perfect vision to gaze at least twenty feet to the bottom. However, our frolicking in the shallows quickly stirred up sediment and dirt from the bottom of the lake, and the clarity diminished.

God's ideal for us includes pure, clean, clear, harmonious, and ultimately enjoyable relationships, like that Mount Rainier lake. Sadly, we have muddied the waters with all sorts of foolery based on the lesser and life-robbing values of this world.

So it is no surprise that as James reveals the description of New Testament wisdom, he begins by saying, "The wisdom from above is first pure." Wisdom is pure and purity is wise.

In James 3:17–18, the purity of wisdom being listed first is not an accident. Purity is preeminent in a wise life. The word *pure* (*hagnos*) refers to innocence and moral blamelessness, also something free of contamination or defilement (just like we want our water, air, and food). In the Greek, *hagnos* is most often translated "holy."

This is the fundamental essence of all gospel wisdom and must be at the core of the other qualities we will examine in the coming pages. Remember, this wisdom is "from above." God, who reigns above, is first holy. As you are reading this page, something truly awesome is concurrently happening "above" that must capture our hearts. The heavenly creatures are surrounding the throne of God in the midst of "flashes of lightning, and rumblings and peals of thunder" (Revelation 4:5). "Day and night they never cease to say, 'Holy, holy, holy, is the Lord God Almighty, who was and is and is to come!'" (Revelation 4:8).

In response to God's holiness, the description follows: "The twenty-four elders fall down before him who is seated on the throne and worship him who lives forever and ever. They cast their crowns before the throne, saying, 'Worthy are you, our Lord and God, to receive glory and honor and power, for you created all things, and by your will they existed and were created'" (Revelation 4:10–11).

In this imagery we see both the priority and power of purity. In the apocryphal book The Wisdom of Solomon, it says that wisdom is “the breath of the power of God, and a pure influence flowing from the glory of the Almighty” (7:25) and “O send her out of thy holy heavens and from the throne of thy glory” (9:10). Jewish writers were agreed that true wisdom came from above, specifically from the glorious throne of a holy God.

Back on earth, we admittedly grovel in this sin-sick and relation-ally broken world. How can we possibly experience and exhibit that kind of wisdom—so pure, so holy?

Throughout history, humankind has recognized the gulf between sinful man and pure deity. Even among the Greeks this was illustrated. The mythical god Aesculapius was the god of healing. Inscribed at the temple dedicated to him in the fourth century BC in the city of Epidaurus, these words appeared: “He who would enter the divine temple must be pure; and purity is to have a mind which thinks holy thoughts.”[2] Holiness preceded healing.

Holy Jesus—Holy Wisdom

True holiness leading to healing has become our reality in Christ. This is only a reasonable proposal, however, if Jesus was himself holy. The wisdom from above is only pure if Jesus was pure. His presence in us is only effective in making us holy if he was sinless.

Six different biblical writers affirm the sinlessness of Jesus. Paul declares that Jesus “knew no sin” (2 Corinthians 5:21). Peter stated that Jesus “committed no sin” (1 Peter 2:22). John said that “in him there is no sin” (1 John 3:5). The writer of Hebrews affirms that Jesus was “tempted in all things as we are, yet without sin” (Hebrews 4:15 NASB). The same writer describes Christ as high priest who is “holy, innocent, unstained, separated from sinners, and exalted above the heavens” (Hebrews 7:26). Psalm 45:7 prophesied that the Messiah would love righteousness and hate wickedness. Isaiah spoke of Jesus as “the righteous one” (Isaiah 53:11).

Jesus himself gave a dramatic confirmation of his sinlessness on the day he faced down the Pharisees and asked, “Which one of you convicts me of sin?” (John 8:46). It has been observed that the im-pact of this moment was not that the Pharisees could not answer the question but that Jesus so courageously asked it. He had just confronted them as sons and subjects of the devil. They had every reason to nail him to the wall. Of course, the disciples knew him intimately and could have piped in with an observation of some slip up, off-color comment, unwholesome display of emotion, or slight hypocrisy in his behavior. As Jerry Bridges has observed, "Yet Jesus dared to ask the question because he knew there was only one answer. He was without sin."[3]

Jesus had to be pure to become the sinless sacrifice for our sins to satisfy God's justice, holiness, and love for the lost souls of men. First Peter 2:24 says of Christ, "He himself bore our sins in his body on the tree, that we might die to sin and live to righteousness. By his wounds you have been healed." Hebrews 10:10 underscores this: "And by that will, we have been made holy through the sacrifice of the body of Jesus Christ once for all" (NIV). A few verses later the writer of Hebrews says, "For by one sacrifice he has made perfect forever those who are being made holy" (10:14 NIV). Pure. Holy. Right before God. Healed. All because of the work of Jesus on the cross.

For those who have been transformed by the gospel, the reality of a pure life before God is possible. The reality of a pure God manifested in our life is promised. First Corinthians 1:30 assures us, "And because of him you are in Christ Jesus, who became to us wisdom from God, righteousness and sanctification and redemption." Notice the life of Jesus' wisdom in combination with his righteousness, sanctification, and redemption—all ours in the fullest—in him. We could say that Christ's pure life in us is the foundation of all the other attributes of wisdom that will be unpacked by James. Granted, we will never be as pure as he is because we are still in this body of "flesh," but the hope of living a distinctive life in a corrupt world is realistic and relevant.

A.W. Tozer responded to the purity of Jesus with this compelling prayer:

> Thou, O Christ, who was tempted in all points like as we are, yet without sin, make us strong to overcome the desire to be wise and to be reputed wise by others as ignorant as ourselves. We turn from our wisdom as well as from our folly and flee to Thee, the wisdom of God and the power of God. Amen.[4]

The Power of a Pure Motive

We all approach relationships with some sense of need. We might feel lonely and in need of a friend. We might simply be looking for a date or even a mate. We might try to find significance by associating with a certain person of perceived importance. In our look-out-for-number-one society, it is common to approach relationships with the wrong motives.

In his letter, James is likely applying this pure wisdom from above to the "teachers" (3:1), who would be judged with greater strictness, whose conduct was not wise and may have been motivated by "jealousy and selfish ambition" (v. 14). In chapter 4 he speaks of their quarrels and fights that sprang from their hearts that were worldly, even though they were masking their impure motives with a veneer of prayer (4:1–14). Those to whom James wrote needed the pure wisdom of God to penetrate "the thoughts and intentions" of their hearts (Hebrews 4:12). Often, we need the same encounter.

I've often said that we can learn more about our motives by our reactions than our actions. Actions can be calculated, whereas reactions are spontaneous, raw, and effectively revealing.

Recently, my wife and I were flying on Christmas Day from Colorado to Virginia to visit family. I had used a credit from a previously cancelled ticket for her flight and award miles for mine. We were flying on the airline I most often use in my ministry travels. Although I had "Executive Platinum" status, we were not on the same itinerary, and my free award ticket did not qualify, so we did not get the customary complimentary upgrade. Being a "travel snob," I reluctantly settled into our coach seats, with a frustrating view of the empty seats in first class.

Just before takeoff, a flight attendant approached and asked, "Are you Mr. Henderson? And is this your wife?" I responded affirmatively, and she continued, "Would you both like to move to first class?" I nodded with a smile. Several people around us blurted out, "Wow! Merry Christmas!" At that point, had my heart been right, I would have expressed humble gratitude. My wife simply said, "What a nice surprise." But because my heart was proud and filled with entitlement, I blurted out, "Well I've earned it—flying 100,000 miles in the last year!" We quickly gathered our things and moved up to the front of the plane.

As soon as we sat down in first class, conviction hit me like a gale force wind. I realized I certainly came across as the most pompous, ungrateful passenger on the plane. I settled into my cushy seat embarrassed, exposed, and exercised that I had so misrepresented the wisdom of Jesus.

My reaction had revealed my true motive. Sadly, it was not gratitude or humility. Rather, it was the ugliness of arrogance and privilege. I needed wisdom from above. Jesus would not have expected first class and would clearly not have reacted as I did at such a kind and undeserved offer.

Often, our reactions—to the jab of a spouse, the criticism of a work associate, the disregard of friends—excite and expose the many ways in which we need a fresh infusion of the wisdom of Jesus that is first pure.

Christ, our wisdom from above, is pure. His holy motives were revealed throughout his earthly ministry. A few headlines about his motives might read:

- "Even the Son of Man came not to be served but to serve, and to give his life a ransom for many" (Mark 10:45).
- "My food is to do the will of him who sent me and to accomplish his work" (John 4:34).
- "The Son can do nothing of his own accord, but only what he sees the Father doing" (John 5:19).
- "Father, I glorified you on earth, having accomplished the work that you gave me to do. . . . I have manifested your name to the people whom you gave me out of the world" (John 17:4, 6).

In summary, it seems that Jesus was motivated to glorify the Father by knowing and accomplishing his will through giving his life away for others.

The apostle Paul—who had been radically changed, lived by Christ's indwelling grace, and wrote inspired Scripture to help us live in wisdom's purity—spoke of pure motives. His motivational CliffsNotes might say:

- "For what we proclaim is not ourselves, but Jesus Christ as Lord, with ourselves as your servants for Jesus' sake" (2 Corinthians 4:5).

- "So whether we are at home or away, we make it our aim to please him" (2 Corinthians 5:9).
- "As it is my eager expectation and hope that I will not be at all ashamed, but that with full courage now as always Christ will be honored in my body, whether by life or by death" (Philippians 1:20).
- "Let each of you look not only to his own interests, but also to the interests of others" (Philippians 2:4).

My paraphrase of what motivated Paul would be that he was driven to please and honor Christ in all things as he proclaimed Christ and put the needs of others before his own. With the purity of those motives in our lives, relationships would improve and flourish, demonstrating wisdom from above.

The Bible proposes something radically distinct from the common acumen of this age in our relational motivation. We find principles like "to have a friend, be a friend." To have your needs met, meet the needs of others. To have influence with others, be their servant.

In my decades of marriage counseling I have discovered that most conflict is rooted in the reality of two broken people, both of whom think the other person is the real problem, neither of whom is willing to change, and each of whom are obsessed with the failure of the other party to meet their personal need. How powerful the pure wisdom from above could be in bringing transformation to marriages, families, friendships, and churches. Tomorrow, as you rise and think of the relationship and routines of daily life, ask for Christ's pure motives to be your primary motives. This is prayer he loves to answer.

The Provision of a Pure Mind

In talking about the pure wisdom from above, the mind matters massively. The Corinthian church was relationally bankrupt, filled with division and conflict. Early in his first letter to them, Paul goes to great lengths to contrast human wisdom (which was at the root of their problems) with the spiritual wisdom found in Christ (1 Corinthians 1:18–2:16). He concludes this argument by saying, "'For who has understood the mind of the Lord so as to instruct him?' But we have the mind of Christ" (2:16). In a later letter he told the Corinthians, "For I feel a divine jealousy for you, since I betrothed you to one husband, to present you as a pure virgin to Christ. But I am afraid that as the serpent deceived Eve by his cunning, your thoughts will be led astray from a sincere and pure devotion to Christ" (2 Corinthians 11:2–3). In a similar vein, Paul challenged the believers at Philippi, "Have this mind among yourselves, which is yours in Christ Jesus" (Philippians 2:5).

Jesus Christ transforms the mind as we abide in him through the grace of the Word and prayer. His life in us changes our will, emotions, behavior, and relationships. Jesus said, "And you will know the truth, and the truth will set you free" (John 8:32). He then declared, "I am the way, and the truth, and the life" (John 14:6). Christ, in whom are hidden all the treasures of wisdom and knowledge, empowers us with a pure mind.

The apostle Paul told us that "to set the mind on the Spirit is life and peace" (Romans 8:6) and "do not be conformed to this world, but be transformed by the renewal of your mind" (Romans 12:2). He also issued this challenge: "Whatever is true, whatever is honorable, whatever is just, whatever is pure, whatever is lovely, whatever is commendable, if there is any excellence, if there is anything worthy of praise, think about these things" (Philippians 4:8).

Our lives are tethered to technology. Because of the threat of viruses and malware, companies that keep our laptops and servers "pure" are in high demand. Wise users regularly run virus and security scans. A wise Christ-follower soon learns to consciously surrender to the mind of Christ as the spiritual and mental virus scan. In the moments of temptation and vulnerability at home, at work, at the mall, or in heated dialogues with a colleague, ask God for the pure mind of Christ. It is a prayer he loves to answer.

The Priority of a Pure Morality

When pure wisdom from above motivates the heart and shapes the thoughts, the result is a morally pure lifestyle. But that's becoming abnormal in our society. We live in a culture where it is funny to be foul-mouthed, cool to be crude, popular to be impure, and alluring to be aberrant.

This reminds me of the story of the dean of a southern college who was reviewing the rules with the freshmen students during orientation. "The female dormitory will be out-of-bounds for all male students, and the male dormitory to the female students. Anybody caught breaking this rule will be fined a hundred dollars the first time." He elaborated, "Anybody caught breaking this rule the second time will be fined two hundred dollars. Anybody being caught a third time will incur a five-hundred-dollar fine. Are there any questions?" In response, a male student in the back raised his hand and inquired, "How much is a season pass?"

Today the culture freely distributes "season passes" to accommodate all imaginable versions of immorality and perversion. When the Ashley Madison hack occurred in 2015, shock waves fanned across the nation into homes and churches with the revelation of the numbers of men who were looking for a "hall pass" to cheat on their wives. Other issues like the redefinition of marriage, the unpopularity of wedding vows versus simply "living together," and the breakup of so many marriages are all indicators of a neglect of the wisdom from above that is "first pure."

The New Testament call is clear. "For this is the will of God, your sanctification: that you abstain from sexual immorality; that each one of you know how to control his own body in holiness and honor. . . . For God has not called us for impurity, but in holiness. Therefore whoever disregards this, disregards not man but God, who gives his Holy Spirit to you" (1 Thessalonians 4:3–8). Ephesians 5:3 underscores the standard, "But sexual immorality and all impurity or covetousness must not even be named among you, as is proper among saints." And again, "The body is not meant for sexual immorality, but for the Lord, and the Lord for the body" (1 Corinthians 6:13). Most of us know the principles of these verses from personal reading or sitting through sermons. But we can experience the power and pure provision to experience these verses through the life of Jesus in us. He is pure. His wisdom imparts purity.

In my all-time favorite devotional, *Thoughts From the Diary of a Desperate Man*, Walter Henrichsen writes,

> God is perfect holiness and when you sin against him, separation results. This Bible calls spiritual death. Sin separates; it always has and always will. Two men are in a partnership where one steals from the other. The result is separation. A husband is unfaithful to his wife and separation occurs. When you sense that your friend has lied to you, an environment of alienation results.[5]

The holy wisdom from above has come to indwell and empower us through Jesus. Relational transformation and healing can trump the separation of sin. Today and every day we must ask, expect, and receive because we know a holy God wants us to live holy lives—with holy motives, holy minds, and a holy morality so that our relationships will adorn the gospel of Jesus Christ.

Titus described the work of Jesus as "the grace of God [that] has appeared, bringing salvation for all people." Then he explains the practical impact of that grace as "training us to renounce ungodliness and worldly passions, and to live self-controlled, upright, and godly lives in the present age." Titus continues in saying that we are "waiting for our blessed hope, the appearing of the glory of our great God and Savior Jesus Christ, who gave himself for us to redeem us from all lawlessness and to purify for himself a people for his own possession who are zealous for good works" (Titus 2:11–14). The power of purity is the indwelling grace of Jesus' life, purifying us for himself. He generously imparts his purity, by grace, when we pray.

Invitation to Drink, Swim, and Satisfy

As we see repeatedly, James' description of wisdom from above runs parallel with Christ's beatitudes on the Sermon on the Mount (Matthew 5:2–12). Jesus announced, "Blessed are the pure in heart, for they shall see God" (5:8). There is no avoiding the fact the sin destroys our souls, relationships, homes, churches, and societies. But there is no question that true happiness prevails when we desire and delight in purity at the core of our being. We will see God. Like the clarity of a swim in pristine Caribbean waters, our vision of Jesus, our experience of his life and his glory, will be lucid. Our assurance of face-to-face eternal worship is certain.

And as Jesus said, his Spirit in us would be like rivers of living water, pure, life-giving, and flowing in and through to satisfy the deepest longings of our thirsty souls (John 7:37–39). He is the pure "spring of water welling up to eternal life" (John 4:14), and we never need to thirst for satisfaction again in the disappointing muddy waters of unholy living in this polluted and sin-sick world. Trust him for this satisfaction and sanctification when you pray. He will purify your motives, your mind, and your moral orientation. It is a prayer he loves to answer because you will be a reflection of his Son in this world and your relationships will be distinctively pure in a morally muddied world.

Ready to Receive

Try to picture the scenes of heaven's worship, described in this chapter. Imagine the holiness of God, the surpassing beauty of the environment, the purity of the hearts, the songs and the praise. Then trust Christ to work in you so that this reality would be demonstrated on earth—and in you—as it is in heaven.

Think about your spontaneous reactions to difficult people and challenging situations during the last week. What do these reveal about the real nature of your motives? Surrender these discoveries to the Lord in hopes of a more pure character of wisdom.

Every time you take a drink of pure water today to provide life for your physical body, think of your need for the pure living water of the life of Jesus. Surrender your soul to his pure, life-giving presence in you, inviting him to impart health and purity to you and though you to others.

Take time to experience the following Wisdom Prayer, allowing the biblical truths to renew your mind as your prayerful response draws your heart closer to Christ, who is your wisdom.

Wisdom Prayer

Pure Jesus

Jesus is our great and sinless high priest who sympathizes with our battles for purity and invites us to receive his mercy and grace in our times of need. His grace is powerful in producing the wisdom from above that is first pure. Two passages that parallel each other will guide our prayer time.

Hebrews 4:14–16

[14] Since then we have a great high priest who has passed through the heavens, Jesus, the Son of God, let us hold fast our confession. [15] For we do not have a high priest who is unable to sympathize with our weaknesses, but one who in every respect has been tempted as we are, yet without sin. [16] Let us then with confidence draw near to the throne of grace, that we may receive mercy and find grace to help in time of need.

Titus 2:11–12

[11] For the grace of God has appeared, bringing salvation for all people, [12] training us to renounce ungodliness and worldly passions, and to live self-controlled, upright, and godly lives in the present age.

REVERENCE—"Who is God?"

Lord Jesus, I praise you because you are . . .

- Great (Hebrews 4:14)
- Our high priest (v. 14)
- Risen and passed through the heavens (v. 14)
- The Son of God (v. 14)
- Sympathetic with my weaknesses (v. 15)
- Sinless though every temptation (v. 15)
- Ruling on a throne of grace (v. 16)

- The giver of mercy (v. 16)
- The giver of grace (v. 16)
- The grace of God that has appeared to men (Titus 2:11)
- Our salvation (v. 11)
- The one who trains us to renounce ungodliness and worldly passions (v. 12)
- The one who trains us to live self-controlled, upright and godly (v. 12)

I praise you, Lord Jesus, that you are my great high priest in heaven, interceding for me when ______________________. (Hebrews 4:14)

I praise you that you were victorious over sin even when you were tempted by ______________________. (Hebrews 4:15)

I thank you that you were sympathetic when I struggled with the weakness of ______________________. (Hebrews 4:15)

RESPONSE—"How should I respond?"

I confess I did not receive your grace when I should have renounced ______________________ [specific struggles with ungodliness and worldly passions]. (Titus 2:12)

REQUESTS—"What should I pray about?"

I sense I am weak today in ______________________ [some area of life] and place my confidence in your mercy and grace to help me ______________________. [Describe what that help would look like.] (Hebrews 4:16)

Today I pray for ______________________ [name] in their time of weakness. Draw them to your throne of grace. (Hebrews 4:16)

Today I will trust your grace to train me to be self-controlled when ______________________. (Titus 2:12)

Today I will trust your grace to train me to be upright and godly when ______________. (Titus 2:12)

READINESS—"Where am I headed?"

Today as I encounter the ungodliness of ______________________________, I will have confidence in your grace to live a pure life. (Titus 2:12)

Today as I might be tempted with evil passions like ____________________________, I will have confidence in your grace to live a pure life. (Titus 2:12)

REVERENCE—"Who is God?"

You are pure and sinless, and by the presence of your Holy Spirit in me, I pray you will allow me to be a testimony of purity to ______________________________ [names]. (Hebrews 4:15)

5

Wisdom Wins in a Culture at War

> But the wisdom from above is . . . peaceable.
>
> James 3:17

> A martyr was fastened to the stake, and the sheriff who was to execute him expressed his sorrow that he should persevere in his opinions and compel him to set fire to the pile. The martyr answered, "Come and lay your hand on my heart, and see if it does not beat quietly." His request was complied with, and he was found to be quite calm. "Now," said he, "lay your hand on your own heart and see if you are not more troubled than I am. Then go your way, and instead of pitying me, pity yourself."
>
> As told by Charles H. Spurgeon

You will remember that the political season leading up to the 2016 presidential elections was anything but normal. Our nation, which has typically valued a peaceable process of voting in order to determine the next POTUS, seemingly was invited to a contentious masquerade party. Angry, intrusive protests; face-punching, out-of-control confrontations; and abusive name-calling all marked the race to the White House. People across the nation and the world were asking, "What is going on in the United States?"

In disgust, many watched the Hollywood-esque drama of the process of determining who would oversee the government that is supposed to bring order and civility to our society. People of all political stripes were disrupting the peace in almost circus-like fashion. This is not just to pick on political candidates and their zealous followers but to illustrate our profound need for a true and transformational peace that quiets hearts, measures dialogue, calms conflict, and promotes genuine understanding in society.

A World of Unrest

It is an understatement to say that we live in a world massively racked by violence and unrest. At a global level, news reports scream stories of societies at war and terrorists groups infiltrating communities to proliferate destruction. We hear heartbreaking stories and see horrific images of innocent people being beheaded, dropped from buildings, and burned alive. Meanwhile, diplomats convene to attempt treaties and ceasefires. In 1945, the United Nations was formed to promote world peace, and since then we've hardly seen a single day of it. I've heard that "peace is that glorious brief moment in history when everyone stops to reload." Truly, the world is in perpetual turbulence.

In grassroots America, racial unrest is not going away. Homicides, murder-suicides, and unlimited variations of other violent expressions are indicative of communities, workplaces, homes, and even marriages—all void of real peace. The court systems are flooded with individuals and corporations trying to find "peaceful" legal resolution for complicated and convoluted conflicts.

In our personal space, peace seems elusive for many. We don't sleep well, anxiety is rampant, and unresolved anger drives millions to relational breakdown, despondency, even depression. Pharmaceutical companies flourish and counselors stay busy as we try to find some new level of well-being.

A Promise for Prevailing Peace

James promised us that the wisdom from above is "peaceable." He underscores the prominent value of peace again in verse 18: "And a harvest of righteousness is sown in peace by those who make peace." Put simply, peace is a vital ingredient of a life that pleases God. In contrast to this, James explained back in 3:16 that a lack of peace is seen in "jealousy and selfish ambition" that produces "disorder and every vile practice." Now there's a summary of much of today's headlines: "Disorder and Every Vile Practice Erupts in Suburbia!" The need for peace is gargantuan.

Peace Delivered

Thomas à Kempis stated, "All men desire peace but very few desire those things that make for peace." Writer Heidi Jo Fulk observed, "We're seeing the results of superficial and temporal peace all around us. While good and necessary action steps have been taken in the past toward peace . . . and good and necessary action steps must still be pursued, they will always fail to bring true, lasting peace if they are not coupled with the truth of the gospel."[1]

Recently, while reflecting during a gospel-centered Good Friday service, I was struck by a phrase from Isaiah 53, the great prophetic passage about Jesus the Messiah, the Suffering Servant. I have read this passage countless times and even memorized it. Yet this phrase captured my heart with fresh intrigue: "Upon him was the chastisement that brought us peace" (v. 5).

The other familiar yet powerful phrases found in this specific verse remind us of the truly amazing blessings that have come through the sacrifice of Christ. "He was pierced for our transgressions; he was crushed for our iniquities . . . and with his wounds we are healed." Praise God for his inexpressible gift to us in the work of Christ!

But notice this again: "Upon him was the chastisement that brought us peace." In the original meaning, peace speaks of completeness, soundness, and well-being. Just as a young mother might experience postpartum depression because of what her body has been through, we can experience peace and become agents of peace because of what his body endured. As I have contemplated our great need for this peace and the incredible work of Christ, a few helpful applications have come to mind.

Sin Destroys Peace

Sin destroyed peace. Sin is the violation of the relationship between man and a holy God—a God of Peace. Sin shattered the perfect divinely created peace of the Garden of Eden. Sin disrupted the first family when Cain killed Abel. For millennia, sin has been the source of troubled hearts, broken marriages, distressed families, divided churches, and warring nations. Behind it all is one who came to "steal and kill and destroy" (John 10:10).

We Cannot Attain Peace

Human efforts to create peace always have and always will fail because no man-made solutions can remove sin. True and lasting peace required the Father's chastisement of our sin, through the substitutionary death of his perfect Son. Forgiveness and transformation of our rebel hearts is now ours in Christ. Permanent, holy cease-fire prevails. Reconciliation of our lives back to God and one another flow from the supernatural source of his life in our blood-washed hearts. This was the only way to provide real and lasting peace. Colossians 1:20 tells us that the Father worked "through him [Christ] to reconcile to himself all things, whether on earth or in heaven, making peace by the blood of his cross."

It is helpful to note that God is not at war with man or fallen angels. They are at war with him. As long as they continue in that war, fueled by sin and rebellion, there will be no peace.

Still, our world groundlessly strives for peace through an abundance of superficial and deficient means. Our leaders concoct treaties, reforms, and resolutions. False teachers offer pithy formulas for "feeling better" and promote positive psychology as a means to peace. This is much like the leaders of Israel in Jeremiah's day, who were greedy for gain and did not want to address the sinful sources behind the lack of personal and national peace. The New Living Translation summarizes it in words so revealing of today's culture: "From the least to the greatest, their lives are ruled by greed. From prophets to priests, they are all frauds. They offer superficial treatments for my people's mortal wound. They give assurances of peace when there is no peace. Are they ashamed of their disgusting actions? Not at all—they don't even know how to blush!" (Jeremiah 6:13–15). One writer comments, "They were like physicians putting bandages over cancer and pronouncing it healed. Their promise of peace was a hollow mockery."[2] Again, only God's solution to sin and our repentance over that sin can bring legitimate and lasting peace.

At an individual level, we pursue temporal relief through relaxation techniques, behavioral modification, vacations, metaphysical therapies, and even drugs and alcohol. Yet real peace is elusive via mere human endeavor apart from God's solution in Christ. "'But the wicked are like the tossing sea; for it cannot be quiet, and its waters toss up mire and dirt. There is no peace,' says my God, 'for the wicked'" (Isaiah 57:20–21). Psalm 28:3 describes them as those who "speak peace with their neighbors while evil is in their hearts." Speaking of humankind's pursuits apart from God, Paul says, "The way of peace they have not known. There is no fear of God before their eyes" (Romans 3:17–18).

The Triune God as the Source of Peace

So how can we find this promised peace in a world that chases after cheap replacements like the frenzied family dog trying to capture a dust devil? In most of the popular versions of the Bible there are about four hundred references to peace. Peace is a major theme and an assured experience for God's people. It could be said that the Bible begins and ends in peace. The dawn of time starts in the serenity of a perfect, God-inhabited garden, untainted by sin. Human history culminates with the reign of "the Prince of peace" and "of the increase of his government and of peace there will be no end" (Isaiah 9:6–7).

Our model for peace is not the image of a happy couple on an isolated beach in one of those all-inclusive tropical vacation commercials.

It is beyond our childhood memories of Christmas Eves gone by when our conflicted family called a temporary truce to try and salvage the holiday. Our model for peace is God himself—Father, Son, and Holy Spirit, living in absolute harmony within a perfect, peaceful union.

Puritan Thomas Watson summarized, "The Father is called the 'God of Peace' (Hebrews 13:20). The Son is called the 'Prince of Peace' (Isaiah 9:6). The Holy Spirit is the Sprit of Peace (Ephesians 4:3). The more a person is peaceable, the more he is like God. . . . Those born of God are peacemakers."[3]

The work of Christ has drawn us back into the original design of finding our well-being in the peace-permeated life and character of the triune God. Martin Goldsmith has written,

> Each of the three persons of the Trinity has a separate identity, yet they live together in unity. They are one, and there is a deep inter-relational harmony. Each person is distinct: the Father is not the Son; and the Son is not the Spirit; and the Spirit is not the Father. And yet despite their separate identities there remains an absolute *shalom*, and absolute harmony and absolute oneness among them.[4]

In Jesus' final extended prayer prior to the cross he said, "The glory that you have given me I have given to them, that they may be one even as we are one, I in them and you in me, that they may become perfectly one, so that the world may know that you sent me and loved them even as you loved me" (John 17:22–23). Jesus prayed of the glory of a triune God, distinct but perfectly one. Different in function but operating in unspoiled peace. Now this glory is ours that we might exhibit a truly peaceable oneness, not only for our own benefit but to authenticate our witness to a world. Christ has made it all visible, palpable, and possible. "For he himself is our peace, who has made us both one and has broken down in his flesh the dividing wall of hostility" (Ephesians 2:14).

Opposites attract in marriage. But the wisdom of his peace can ensure us against opposites that attack. Family members can rub each other the wrong way, but the life of God enables us to relate the right way, beyond the differences of personality and opinion. Churches are filled with diverse temperaments, backgrounds, opinions, and aspirations. But when we are a people of prayer, we drink of something more delightful than our petty differences. Our great and generous God fills us with the mind and heart of Christ, that we might manifest the wisdom from above that is peaceable. In every relationship we need more light and less heat. More of the light of his peaceable wisdom; less of the heat of our earthly opinions and self-centered emotions.

Agents of His Peace

Jesus linked our very identity and role in this world with the reality of peace. "Blessed are the peacemakers, for they shall be called sons of God" (Matthew 5:9). As is commonly noted, "blessed" means truly happy. The term *sons of God* speaks of dignity and honor. This verse is not just talking about the affection involved in being a son of God, although that reality is profound. Rather, this speaks about the dignity and honor of being a son of God.

We use a lot of superficial descriptors to label ourselves. Some contradict our true identity as "peacemakers." We use terms like *hotheaded*, *short-fused*, *type-A*, *pot-stirrer*, or *in-your-face*. These may be occasional behaviors, but they are not our identity. Next time you look in the mirror, say to yourself, "You are a peacemaker, a child of the God of Peace, a subject of the Prince of Peace, and indwelt by his Spirit of Peace." Don't forget who you are.

The Father has given us the name "peacemaker." It is indeed a worthy name to bear, one to be guarded wisely. May we exhibit this core identity to our children, friends, and associates as those who are truly living by the wisdom from above that is peaceable.

As we wear the label "child of God," we honor the Father's expectations. The New Testament commands a testimony of peaceableness with all (Romans 12:18; Hebrews 12:14). We are to prioritize prayer in the church so "that we may lead a peaceful and quiet life, godly and dignified in every way" (1 Timothy 2:2). As we live by God's wisdom rather than the world's, we will be peaceable and demonstrate the truth that "a harvest of righteousness is sown in peace by those who make peace" (James 3:17–18). Most literally, James tells us that a person living in wisdom is "peace-loving."

Grace Provides Amazing Peace

We must remember that on a continual basis, it is only the undeserved favor of God in Christ that has, does, and will provide ultimate peace. Our need for peace compels us to cast ourselves daily upon the grace of God to do in us, for us, and through us what only Christ can do. It is notable that throughout the New Testament, the dual greeting and benediction of "grace and peace" are reiterated not as a throw-away phrase, but as the core need of every Christ-follower. In every letter Paul and Peter wrote, they began with the blessing and prayer "Grace and peace."

As you wake up each morning in a conflicted home environment, pray with a conscious and concrete affirmation for his "grace and peace." As you walk into a tense office environment tomorrow, whisper the prayer, "Grace and peace." In those moments of emotional escalation as you diffuse an angry conversation with your teenager, let your heart run to the throne of grace and receive his provision of "grace and peace." We must remember every day (and every minute of every day) that we cannot achieve peace. Rather, we must *receive* peace. The Prince of Peace has endless provision and loves to answer your prayer for the wisdom that is peaceable.

Clearly, peace does not operate from the outside in, rather from the inside out. As has often been said, "Peace is not the absence of conflict. Rather, it is the presence of Christ." He is the great Prince of Peace. Thus, peace is not trumped by our circumstances. His peace transcends our circumstances. The fruit of the life of the Spirit of Christ within us is peace (Galatians 5:22). Jesus promised that the peace he gives us is not like the world's (dependent on externals), but rather is rooted in his overcoming life in us (John 14:27).

Peace, If Possible

We must be diligent to do all we do with a passion for godly peace. Romans 12:18 says, "If possible, so far as it depends on you, live peaceably with all." We are all comforted by the "if possible" disclaimer, because the possibilities can be tested by others who are in a bad mood or affected by illness or are characteristically cantankerous.

In the cartoon series *Peanuts* is a boy nicknamed Pigpen, who is noted for his ever-filthy overalls and the cloud of dirt and dust that follows him around. When he takes a deep breath or moves in the slightest, the dust rises around him. He seems to take pride in the cloud that surrounds him, referring to it as the dust of ancient civilizations. He seems to have no ability to stay clean. In an early cartoon strip, it joked that Pigpen was the only person who could get dirty while walking in a snowstorm.[5]

Similar to Pigpen, we know some people can promote conflict while stranded on a desert island. They are over-the-top dysfunctional, willfully unforgiving, and habitually negative and agitated. Interacting with them makes peace difficult. But this does not excuse us. We should pray for them, trusting God for an eventual breakthough that would address the core pain behind their conflicted life. We must also own our personal attitudes and responses, surrender to Christ, and seek to live peaceably with all. One day we will give an account for our love for peace, not their lack of peace.

Peace Preserves

Ultimately we must not disrupt God's established and ideal state of affairs. He desired and designates peace as the default environment for his children. In Ephesians 4:1–3, Paul provided the game plan for one who "makes peace":

> Walk in a manner worthy of the calling to which you have been called, with all humility and gentleness, with patience, bearing with one another in love, eager to maintain the unity of the Spirit in the bond of peace.

So whenever peace is disrupted, it is safe to say that someone is not walking worthy of Christ and his calling on their life. Someone is violating humility. Someone is being impatient. Someone is not lovingly giving of themselves to others in genuine love. Someone is "disturbing the peace" that the Holy Spirit always establishes. Someone is not asking in faith for the wisdom from above. Someone is not living consistent with the peace and unity of our triune God (see Ephesians 4:4–7). Don't be that someone. Instead, be the one who pursues "what makes for peace and for mutual upbuilding" (Romans 14:19).

Word and Prayer

One of my more memorable conversations occurred on a Sunday afternoon as I stood by a small river with a church member named Dale. He was a Bible teacher, often leading a large Sunday school class at his church. That day I had been blessed by one of his profound lessons but was surprised to learn that, for many years earlier in his life, he had wandered far from the Lord. Surprised, I asked how this happened. His answer has been etched in my mind ever since. He said, "The Christian life is like this river. We are swimming upstream in a downstream world—and there are two strokes. The Word and prayer. All I had to do to get washed downstream was to quit stroking."

Our resolve to be peaceable is confronted continually by the downstream forces of conflict, anger, and disruption. But by the graces of God's Word and prayer, we can move onward, regardless of the surrounding torrents that confront us.

Gideon was a man prone to fear and often void of peace. When God called this unlikely leader to deliver Israel from the oppression of the pagan tribes of Midian, Gideon deferred to his insecurities. On numerous occasions God showed his miraculous power to Gideon to bolster his faith and obedience. In one meeting, the Lord appeared to him, an encounter Gideon described as seeing the angel of the Lord "face to face." The text reads, "Then the Lord said to him, 'Peace be to you. Do not fear; you shall not die.' Then Gideon built an altar there to the Lord and called it, The LORD IS PEACE" (Judges 6:23–24).

Every day we have the privilege of revisiting the altar of Gideon, where, like him, we receive the word of the Lord in a face-to-face encounter. Psalm 119:165 promises, "Great peace have those who love your law; nothing can make them stumble." Over the years, when praying for parishioners going into surgery, I have often quoted Isaiah

26:3: "You keep him in perfect peace whose mind is stayed on you, because he trusts in you." The best way to keep our mind stayed on God's character, resulting trust, and peace is by meditation on the truth of his character revealed in his Word.

The New Testament promises this assurance: "And let the peace of Christ rule in your hearts, to which indeed you were called in one body. And be thankful. Let the word of Christ dwell in you richly, teaching and admonishing one another in all wisdom, singing psalms and hymns and spiritual songs, with thankfulness in your hearts to God" (Colossians 3:15–16). Whether we experience the word of Christ in community with family and fellow believers or in our private time in the Scriptures, that very pursuit of the word of Christ unleashes the rule of the peace of Christ.

Similarly, we have this gospel promise: "And the peace of God, which surpasses all understanding, will guard your hearts and your minds in Christ Jesus" (Philippians 4:7). The idea of this peace-guardian is a military term assuring us that God's peace will be a defense force around our inner senses and thoughts. Like Roman military garrisons that were stationed to guard the *Pax Romana* or like a modern-day peacekeeping force, we can experience peace.

How does this peace ensue in our lives? Paul tells us, "Do not be anxious about anything, but in everything by prayer and supplication with thanksgiving let your requests be made known to God" (Philippians 4:6). Seeking God's face and trusting him with our concerns provides supernatural tranquility of soul. This is a prayer God loves to answer.

Forfeited Peace?

Joseph Scriven lived a wealthy, educated, and privileged life in Ireland. But tragedy unexpectedly entered when, on the night before his wedding, his fiancée drowned. God used this pain to draw him closer to Christ.

Scriven decided to change his lifestyle. He left Ireland for Port Hope, Canada, intent on spending his days helping others in greater need. In time, he became known as the Good Samaritan of Port Hope.

When Scriven's mother became very ill in Ireland, he sent a poem he had written, in hopes of providing comfort in her final days. Later, when Scriven was himself very ill, a friend came by to visit. During the visit, he saw the words to that same poem scribbled on scratch paper near Scriven's bed. He asked, "Who wrote those beautiful words?" Scriven replied, "The Lord and I did it between us."[6] The poem began:

> What a friend we have in Jesus, all our sins and griefs to bear!
> What a privilege to carry everything to God in prayer!
> O what peace we often forfeit, O what needless pain we bear
> All because we do not carry everything to God in prayer.[7]

The God of Peace Wins!

Our confidence in the character of God assures us that his peace is an overcoming reality in this troubled and evil world. Writing to persecuted Christians in Thessalonica, Paul affirmed, "Now may the Lord of peace himself give you peace at *all* times in *every* way" (2 Thessalonians 3:16). The writer of Hebrews concluded his letter by assuring the readers that "the God of peace who brought again from the dead our Lord Jesus" would surely "equip you with *everything* good that you may do his will, working in us that which is pleasing in his sight" (Hebrews 13:20–21). Let this strong assurance fill you with hope: "The God of peace will soon crush Satan under your feet" (Romans 16:20). Priscilla Shirer describes our assurance this way, "When we talk about the peace of God, don't think of singing and swaying and holding hands in a circle. The peace of God is strong, intense, palpable, real. You can sense its stable presence giving you inner security despite insecure circumstances."[8]

Your Legacy of Peace

The world remembers Alfred Nobel as the originator of the Nobel Peace Prize. But in 1888, eight years before his death, a French newspaper mistook the death of his brother, Ludvig, for his. The headline read, "The Merchant of Death is Dead." The article recounted, "Dr. Alfred Nobel, who made his fortune by finding a way to kill the most people as ever before in the shortest time possible, died yesterday." During the bulk of his career, Nobel was notably famous for the invention of dynamite and was criticized broadly for its destructive affects. His premature obituary devastated Nobel. He wanted to be known as a man of peace. He quickly realized that if his obituary was to be rewritten, he would have to change the nature of his life. He subsequently changed his will, bequeathing most of his massive fortune to the establishment of a series of prizes, so that no future obituary writer would have any doubt as to his yearning for peace and progress.[9]

Today may be your day for a change. The God of Peace waits for your call that he might rule your life by the presence of the Prince of Peace. May "Rest in Peace" be more than a superficial etching on a tombstone. May it be the current reputation and impact of your life! Wise. Peaceable. Like Jesus.

Ready to Receive

Remember today that real peace is not achieved, but received. Think of peace as a priceless gift purchased by the precious blood of Jesus. With open hands and a surrendered heart, thank him for the price that was paid for the privilege of peace, and know that he gave his all so that he can give this peace to you right now.

As you endeavor to live as a peacemaker today, imagine that your model is the perfect peace of the triune God (God of Peace, Prince of Peace, Spirit of Peace). Keep your heart set on this empowering model as you transcend the trouble and turbulence of the world you face day after day.

Remember the paramount New Testament theme of "grace and peace" in the coming days. In those moments when you sense the need, let your heart cry out, "God give me grace to be at peace with ____________________." Expect his grace to be sufficient.

Take time to experience the following Wisdom Prayer, allowing the biblical truths to renew your mind as your prayerful response draws your heart closer to Christ, who is your wisdom.

Wisdom Prayer

Peace That Overcomes

In the final moments of his Upper Room dialogue with the disciples, Jesus spoke somewhat figuratively of his coming death and resurrection. He described their coming sorrow but also their eventual, great joy. He also explained their new access to the Father in his name. We pick up the conversation in the following verses, focusing only on the words of Jesus.

John 16:25–28, 32–33

25 “I have said these things to you in figures of speech. The hour is coming when I will no longer speak to you in figures of speech but will tell you plainly about the Father. 26 In that day you will ask in my name, and I do not say to you that I will ask the Father on your behalf; 27 for the Father himself loves you, because you have loved me and have believed that I came from God. 28 I came from the Father and have come into the world, and now I am leaving the world and going to the Father. . . . 32 Behold, the hour is coming, indeed it has come, when you will be scattered, each to his own home, and will leave me alone. Yet I am not alone, for the Father is with me. 33 I have said these things to you, that in me you may have peace. In the world you will have tribulation. But take heart; I have overcome the world.”

REVERENCE—“Who is God?”

Lord Jesus, I praise you because . . .

- You have revealed the Father (vv. 25, 28)

- Your work and name give us access in prayer (v. 26)
- You have shown us the love of the Father (v. 27)
- You have brought us to love and believe in you (v. 27)
- You have risen and gone to the Father (v. 28)
- You came into our world with the gospel (v. 28)
- You model how we can handle rejection and loneliness (v. 32)
- In you and your Word we have peace (v. 33)
- You have overcome the world (v. 33)

I praise you, Lord Jesus, that your life has shown us that the Father is ____________________________. (vv. 25, 28)

Lord Jesus, I love you because ____________________________. (v. 27)

Lord Jesus, I believe in you because ____________________________. (v. 27)

RESPONSE—"How should I respond?"

I confess that, like the disciples, when hostility and tribulation caused them to leave you, I have not stood for you when ________________________. Give me peace and courage to always stand for the gospel.

REQUESTS—"What should I pray about?"

Father, because of your love for me in Christ, I pray in his name (consistent with his character and gospel) that you will ____________________________________. (vv. 26–27)

"Prince of Peace," give me overcoming peace today in my relationship with ____________________. (v. 33)

"Prince of Peace," give me overcoming peace today as I encounter ________________________. (v. 33)

I pray for ______________________________(name), who is experiencing loneliness. May they have a great awareness of your presence bringing comfort and peace today. (v. 32)

READINESS—"Where am I headed?"

Even though this world is filled with tribulations like ____, I have peace in knowing you have overcome the world. (v. 33)

REVERENCE—"Who is God?"

Lord Jesus, because you have risen and gone to the Father, you will overcome ________________________________. (vv. 28, 33)

6

Gentle Wisdom—Still in Style

But the wisdom from above is . . . gentle.

James 3:17

I choose gentleness . . . Nothing is won by force.
I choose to be gentle. If I raise my voice may it be only in praise.
If I clench my fist, may it be only in prayer.
If I make a demand, may it be only of myself.[1]

Max Lucado

Have you ever been told you are opinionated or dogmatic? Do you ever use guilt, coercion, intimidation, or threats to get your children to obey, your colleagues to comply, or your friends to cooperate? Do you ever feel threatened by opposite personalities or find yourself resenting people who disagree with you? If so, this is a good time to start praying in faith and with consistency for the gentle wisdom that God wants to give you in Christ. He is gentle. Through his wisdom you will be stronger and your relationships can be helped and healed by the grace of gentleness. And men, this is not just a chapter for women!

There is no question: We are all doing life in an aggressive, competitive, in-your-face culture. The strong, the controlling, the dominant personalities of society, business, and even religion seem to be the ones who get ahead in this life. In a dog-eat-dog world, no one wants to be the weaker dog.

It is interesting that the animal kingdom boasts numerous species that are known as "gentle giants." Manatees, found in Florida and other parts of the Caribbean, weigh over one thousand pounds and eat almost 150 pounds of vegetation a day. In spite of their size, tourists converge in the warm waters to swim with these calm and fascinating creatures, also known as sea cows. The whale shark can grow to 32 feet in length and weigh up to 20,000 pounds. They have 300 to 350 rows of teeth, yet they have posed no threat to humans and have allowed people to swim and interact with them without incident.

Back on land, Clydesdale horses, the mastiff dog, silver mountain gorillas, giraffes, and even elephants are identified as gentle giants. These creatures are ominous in size but characterized by a calm and mellow demeanor. The idea of a gentle giant presumes that the very strength and size of a being is what enables them to stop throwing their weight around and interrelate with respect and confidence.

The great "giant" of human history who is all-powerful and truly awesome, laureled as the King of Kings and Lord of Lords, described himself as "gentle and humble in heart" (Matthew 11:29 NIV). He said that in him we would experience rest, not stress. We would find revitalization, not intimidation or competition. His humble and meek attitude was demonstrated as he served others instead of seeking to exhibit some superficial superiority to them. His gentleness flowed from a spirit of real love for the individual—and ultimate concern for individuals and their well-being.

Christ-followers ought to be known as the "gentle giants" of the world. We are indwelt by the greatness of God yet able to express the secure, considerate, self-controlled gentleness of Christ. A powerful ocean can produce a gentle breeze that captures the mind with the awe of the magnitude of the sea while leaving the senses calmed by the beauty of the shore.

Massive Tenderness

I once attended a conference where the host pastor told a story of one of his volunteers who worked in the church nursery. Unsuspecting mothers would come to the door prepared to hand their precious children over to a kindly middle-aged lady or another young mom. Instead, they were greeted by an ominous, muscular man who had been known as "the heart of the defense" for the Chicago Bears—known as the Monsters of the Midway—in the mid-1980s. His name? Mike Singletary. This Hall of Fame linebacker was providing gentle, attentive care to the babies of the church. He was not less "manly" as he portrayed a caring demeanor. He was serving like Christ. This reminded me of the apostle Paul who described his strong, spiritual influence on the believers in the church at Thessalonica: "But we were gentle among you, like a nursing mother taking care of her own children" (1 Thessalonians 2:7).

What Is Gentleness?

Dutch Reformed Pastor George W. Bethune wrote, "Perhaps no grace is less prayed for, or less cultivated than gentleness. Indeed, it is considered rather as belonging to natural disposition or external manner, than as a Christian virtue; and seldom do we reflect that not to be gentle is sin."[2] So what is this often-ignored character quality of gentleness?

A simple definition tells us that gentleness is "sensitivity of disposition and kindness of behavior, founded on strength and prompted by love."[3] The *New Bible Dictionary* describes it as the "condescension of the divine Judge, whose refusal to exact the full demands of the law lifts up those who would otherwise be crushed under its condemnation."[4] God, who is all powerful, awesome, and a perfect judge, deals with us gently, lifting us up rather than throwing us down as we often deserve.

Psalm 18:35 says, "You have given me the shield of your salvation, and your right hand supported me, and your gentleness made me great." The original NIV (1984) translated it as "You stoop down to make me great." Author Jerry Bridges comments, "Gentleness is stooping down to help someone. God continually stoops down to help us, and he wants us to do the same—to be sensitive to the rights and feelings of others."[5] Billy Graham has described it as "mildness in dealing with others . . . a sensitive regard for others and is careful never to be unfeeling for the rights of others."[6]

Gentleness is closely related to the quality of meekness—which is not to be confused with weakness, but is rather a disciplined strength. Again, Bridges clarifies, "Gentleness is an active trait, describing the manner in which we should treat others. Meekness is a passive trait, describing the proper Christian response when others mistreat us. . . . Both gentleness and meekness are born of power, not weakness."[7] Gentleness evokes the image of a beautiful, strong stallion, trained under bit and bridle. The stallion retains all his tremendous strength but now operates under the control of a master.

Greek scholar W. E. Vine elaborates on our source for gentleness when he describes it as a "grace of the soul; and the exercises of it are first and chiefly towards God. It is that temper of spirit in which we accept his dealings with us as good, and therefore without disputing or resisting."[8] Vine reminds us that our ability to exhibit gentleness starts with our view of God and our response to him. Our security, rooted in his dealings with us, provides a security in our dealings with others.

As Vine states, this quality "manifested by the Lord and commended to the believer is the fruit of power. . . . the Lord was 'meek' because he had the infinite resources of God at his command." Finally, he says that biblical gentleness is "neither elated nor cast down, simply because it is not occupied with self at all."[9] So real gentleness is the mark of a secure and selfless heart, ruled by the character of Jesus Christ.

Who Needs to Be Gentle?

In our culture of winning-by-intimidation workplaces and assertiveness training in most realms of business, gentleness is just not esteemed as an important ingredient for leadership and effectiveness. However, the Bible is clear about the virtue of gentleness. So who needs to pray for gentleness?

Church leaders are required to be gentle as a qualification for their role (1 Timothy 3:3). Later in 1 Timothy it says that a man of God must pursue gentleness (1 Timothy 6:11). In 2 Timothy 2:24, Paul further states that a servant of the Lord must not quarrel but be "gentle to all" (2 Timothy 2:24 NKJV). This might change the dynamic of a lot of church leadership teams and staff cultures.

But it is not just church leaders. Every believer must exhibit gentleness. It is a necessary attitude to restore a sinning brother (Galatians 6:1). Our witness to non-Christians is most fruitful when we communicate with gentleness and respect (2 Timothy 2:25; 1 Peter 3:15). Our love for one another must exhibit an attitude of being completely gentle (Ephesians 4:2). We are commanded to "clothe ourselves" with gentleness (Colossians 3:12 NIV) and are told that the fruit of the Spirit includes a supernatural display of gentleness (Galatians 5:22–23). Philippians 4:5 (NIV) says that our gentleness should be evident to all. Wives who desire to win their unbelieving husbands are encouraged to do so by demonstrating "the imperishable beauty of a gentle and quiet spirit" (1 Peter 3:4).

The writer Matthew describes our Lord in these words: "Behold, your king is coming to you, humble, and mounted on a donkey. . . ." (Matthew 21:5). The apostle Paul writes, "By the humility and gentleness of Christ, I appeal to you" (2 Corinthians 10:1 NIV). Do people expect us to come to them in gentleness? When we are passionate to get a point across, do others get the impression that we are communicating in the humility and gentleness of Christ?

The Competitive Alternative

In contrast to this quality of gentleness, I remember asking a friend about the new pastor of his church. His first response was, "I like him. He is a real competitor. I've played basketball with him several times; he's aggressive and has a temper." I grew up playing competitive sports and still enjoy them. However, to hear this ideal described as a primary trait of a Christian leader gave me cause for a reconsideration of the biblical standards of leadership.

Granted, the New Testament does talk about us being in a contest—an intense war. The apostle Paul used athletic and military terms to describe the Christian life and spiritual leadership. He taught that we are in competition with a spiritual enemy over the eternal destiny of souls. There is a place for "righteous indignation" toward sin and the dishonoring of God's Word and character, like the scene of Christ casting money-changers out of the Temple.

Yet the idea of being a "competitor" in order to gratify our ego with a win over some inferior human is far removed from New Testament leadership. Intimidation through anger in order to assert our will in some selfish battle of personalities is not affirmed in Scripture. At the root of this drive is pride, often fueled by insecurity.

We compete in subtle ways in everyday life. A husband comes home speaking of how tired he is from endless meetings. The wife counters with comments about how wearisome it was taking care of unruly children all day. Thus commences the "my-day-can-beat-your-day" contest. He elaborates on the traffic, the unreasonable boss, the broken air-conditioning in the car. She expresses compiled frustration about the cat drinking from the toilet, the malfunctioning dishwasher, and the burned casserole. Neither is under the impression that the other is listening or really gives a flying leap about concerns other than their own.

Of course, gentleness by either party would defer with a sense of the Lord's strength and sufficiency for the personal frustrations of the day. They could then focus instead on the feelings of the other spouse. I know I am meddling now, but most couples could use a divine dose of this wisdom from above, as the lack of real gentleness is one of the greatest problems in marriage.

One writer notes, "True meekness may be a quality of the strong, those who could assert themselves but choose not to do so. The strong . . . who decline to domineer. Self-assertion is never a Christian virtue; rather, it is Christian to be busy in lowly service and to refuse to engage in the conduct that merely advances one's personal aims."[10] In *Mere Christianity*, C. S. Lewis wrote, "Pride . . . is competitive by its very nature. . . . Pride gets no pleasure out of having something, only out of having more of it than the next man. We say that people are proud of being rich, or clever, or good-looking, but they are not. They are proud of being richer, or more clever, or better-looking than others. . . . Once the element of competition has gone, pride has gone."[11]

The Balance

There is a fine line between striving for excellence and competitive pride—just as there may be a fine line between gentleness and weakness. But there is a wide divide between a gentle spirit and a competitive spirit in our spiritual journey. One is the fruit of security and selflessness while the other is evidence of insecurity, self-absorption, and pride.

I remember hearing the story of a young dad making pancakes one morning for his two boys—Robert, the older, and Ryan, a year younger. As the pancakes came off the griddle, the boys argued about who would get the first serving. The dad interjected, "Boys, if Jesus were sitting here, what would he say?" He clarified, "He would say, 'Let my brother have the first pancake, I can wait.'" At this, Robert blurted, "Okay, Ryan—you be Jesus."

Too often we expect the other person to be the gentle Jesus. It is easy to make excuses. Sometimes we can think that gentleness is a personality trait, but we must embrace it as a Christlike trait. We might think of it as a special gift that only some receive, but it is a holy calling that all of us must embrace. We might be guilty of pursuing other "more important" virtues like love, joy, or peace—forgetting that gentleness is just as vital as a characteristic of Christ, an expression of his spirit, and an essential mark of a wise life.

Jesus calls us to his wisdom as he extends this invitation: "Take my yoke upon you. Let me teach you, because I am humble and gentle at heart, and you will find rest for your souls. For my yoke is easy to bear, and the burden I give you is light" (Matthew 11:29–30 NLT). I am captured by the statement "gentle at heart." For the Christian, gentleness is not the result of an external behavior modification. It is the fruit of a heart transformed and ruled by Christ.

I heard of a woman who was having car problems. It seemed her car was not stopping properly, and she suspected a malfunction with her brakes. After a visit to the repair shop, the mechanic told her, "I couldn't fix your brakes, so I just made your horn louder." We must trust the Lord to address the real issues of our heart. Just moving ahead with a louder horn, or some new resolve to monitor our horn usage, is not a Christ-honoring answer.

Recently I was engaged in a conversation with a group of brothers as we discussed a meeting we had just concluded. I asked one of the guys if he felt I had been too forceful in interjecting my opinions. He responded, "Not at all. You're a gentle spirit." I was shocked, maybe even embarrassed. I have always been a type-A driver with strong opinions and a dominant personality. I really was not sure what to think about being called "gentle." Maybe I am just getting soft as I get older. Maybe I was just having an off day. Perhaps I am becoming more Christlike in a fashion that eclipses my natural personality. I hope so. One thing is for sure: In spite of the machismo masquerade men in our society tend to portray, I need a clear and compelling understanding the wisdom that is gentle, and I need to pray for it every day.

Ask and He Will Give

As we pray for the gentleness of wisdom, here are a few reminders to help us receive that which our Father longs to give to us in Christ. Our receiving is rooted by faith in his character. This is the confidence of our prayers.

Gentleness in Greatness

Our prayer should always begin with worship, according to the model given to us by Christ. Our Father in heaven, whose name is holy, is perfectly gentle. We often do not register this on the top of the list of our points of praise.

Isaiah 40:9–31 contains some familiar verses. This is a section of Isaiah's book, often titled "The Greatness of God." In these verses, Isaiah declares, "Behold your God!" then goes on to exalt God as a mighty ruler who recompenses evil. He controls the elements of the earth in glorious power. He is all-wise beyond any counsel of men. He sits above the circle of the earth, bringing princes to nothing and merely blowing on the kingdoms of this world to upend them. He is the creator of the ends of the earth. More could be said—and Isaiah said it. Our God is indeed an awesome God.

But embedded in this passage we find an amazing contrasting statement: "He will tend his flock like a shepherd; he will gather the lambs in his arms; he will carry them in his bosom, and gently lead those that are with young" (Isaiah 40:11). This is a picture of a tender, caring, and condescending God—with a gentleness born out of his matchless greatness.

I often quote A.W. Tozer, who said, "What comes into our minds when we think about God is the most important thing about us."[12] Today as you worship God, don't forget to exalt his gentleness—then pray that his character would be exalted in how you act and react, speak and listen, give and receive—hour by hour and day by day.

Gentle Shepherd

When we pray, we can also turn our eyes upon Jesus in humble adoration for his gentle character and life. One of the tender and serene images of biblical times is that of a shepherd caring, guiding, and providing for his sheep.

Jesus was the fulfillment of the Old Testament shepherd who knew his flocks and paid careful attention to their welfare (Proverbs 27:23) and rescued them from danger (Amos 3:12). He is the one who would seek after the lost sheep (Ezekiel 34:12). It was Jesus who was prophesied about in Micah 5:2 (NIV): "But you Bethlehem, in the land of Judah . . . for out of you will come a ruler who will be called the shepherd of my people." Of course, Jesus is the personification of the Lord who is our shepherd, portrayed in Psalm 23.

A popular chorus from years ago declared him to be the "gentle shepherd" who we desperately need to feed us and help us find our way.[13] Another classic hymn says:

> Savior, like a shepherd lead us,
> Much we need Thy tender care;
> In Thy pleasant pastures feed us,
> For our use Thy folds prepare:
> Blessed Jesus, blessed Jesus,
> Thou hast bought us, Thine we are;
> Blessed Jesus, blessed Jesus,
> Thou hast bought us, Thine we are.[14]

His shepherd's heart is seen in Matthew 9:36, where we read, "When he saw the crowds, he had compassion on them because they were confused and helpless, like sheep without a shepherd" (NLT). For so many reasons we can understand why Christ is called the Good Shepherd (John 10), the Chief Shepherd (1 Peter 5:4), and the Great Shepherd (Hebrews 13:20).

The passage that has most inspired me to adore and surrender to Jesus as my Gentle Shepherd is 1 Peter 2:21–25. Read it and I think you will understand why.

> For to this you have been called, because Christ also suffered for you, leaving you an example, so that you might follow in his steps. He committed no sin, neither was deceit found in his mouth. When he was reviled, he did not revile in return; when he suffered, he did not threaten, but continued entrusting himself to him who judges justly. He himself bore our sins in his body on the tree, that we might die to sin and live to righteousness. By his wounds you have been healed. For you were straying like sheep, but have now returned to the Shepherd and Overseer of your souls.

This is the Jesus in whom are hidden all the treasures of wisdom and knowledge. We are called to walk in his steps of secure and enduring trust. At the most unjust, pain-inflicted, shameful, and horrific moments of his life he astounds the world with gentle trust in the justice of his Father. We find no hint of severity or aroma of retaliation toward his corrupt persecutors and violent executioners. Jesus, resolutely bound for the cross, is the ultimate picture of strength under control. He could have called myriads of angels to his aid, but in love he endured the cross, disregarding its shame. In impeccable gentleness, the shepherd laid down his life for his sheep—straying, disobedient, ungrateful sheep at that. And because of his sacrifice, we now return to this great and gentle "shepherd and overseer" of our very souls. We ask him for wisdom to live as he lived. With a model like that, how can we not pray for wisdom from above that is so profoundly gentle?

This kind of intentional, submissive discipleship has great reward. Jesus said, "Blessed are the meek [gentle], for they shall inherit the earth" (Matthew 5:5). The assertive and overbearing personalities in this world live by the motto "Get all you can, and can all you get," often at the expense of relationships. Sadly, their "can" of aggressive accolades and accumulations will prove to rattle like the sound of a lone kernel of popcorn at the bottom of the jar. They have their reward.

I've often joked, "The early bird may get the worm but the second mouse gets the cheese." Domineering approaches may get the first touchdown, but gentleness wins in eternity, where the only enduring scoreboard resides. Nancy DeMoss Wolgemuth has noted,

> The world esteems just the opposite of meekness—self-assertiveness, stand up for your rights, be demanding, speak your mind, have it your way. God highly values the things that the world despises. The world looks at meek people and says, "They're weak." God looks at meek people and says, "They remind me of Jesus." God highly values meekness and the world detests it and despises it, but the world highly esteems and values what God detests.[15]

Gentleness Does

As we close, let's review the behaviors of gentleness in some practical terms. We must live each day in anticipation of the opportunities to demonstrate the gentle character of God, model of Christ, and fruit of the Spirit.

Jerry Bridges reminds us that gentleness "will first include actively seeking to make others feel at ease, or 'restful,' in our presence."[16] Opinionated, dogmatic, guilt-inducing communication is just not worthy of the wisdom from above. Christian gentleness will also exhibit respect for the personal dignity of the other person. In interpersonal dialogue, gentleness will persuade the behavior or opinions of others with gracious reason and kindness, not by domination or intimidation.

Gentleness also filters blunt and terse speech. Bridges notes, "Gentle Christians do not feel that they have the liberty to 'say what I think and let the chips fall where they may.' . . . When they find it necessary to wound with words, they also seek to bind up those wounds with words of consolation and encouragement."[17] Proverbs 15:1 reminds us, "A gentle answer turns away wrath, but a harsh word stirs up anger" (NASB).

Finally, Bridges again exhorts, "Gentle Christians will not degrade or belittle or gossip about the brother or sister who falls into some sin. Instead they will grieve for him or her and pray for the person's repentance."[18] True spiritual wisdom will not allow us to shoot our wounded but rather "restore him in a spirit of gentleness." And as Paul says, the Christ-follower will "keep watch on yourself, lest you too be tempted" (Galatians 6:1).

With this in mind, think of the people in your family, circle of friends, professional network, and church that could use the honoring and healing impact of your gentle behavior. Then resolve to live each day with gratitude for the many ways our generous and gentle God has carried us in his arms. Embrace Jesus, who is humble and gentle in heart. Surrender to his Spirit in us, which produces gentle behavior as the evidence of his life. In this way we will show that we are truly wise and understanding, showing by our good behavior that our deeds are done "in the gentleness of wisdom" (James 3:13 NASB).

One of Aesop's fables, *The North Wind and the Sun*, illustrates the value of gentleness well:

> Once upon a time when everything could talk, the Wind and the Sun fell into an argument as to which was the stronger. Finally they decided to put the matter to a test; they would see which one could make a

> certain man, who was walking along the road, throw off his cape. The Wind tried first. He blew and he blew. The harder and colder he blew, the tighter the traveler wrapped his cape about him. The Wind finally gave up and told the Sun to try. The Sun began to smile and as it grew warmer and warmer, the traveler was comfortable once more. But the Sun shone brighter and brighter until the man grew so hot the sweat poured out of his face, he became weary, and seating himself on a stone, he quickly threw his cape to the ground.[19]

The moral of the story is that persuasion is better than force. Gentleness had accomplished what intensity could not.

The bottom line is that we must live and relate to others from the strength and security that is only found in Christ. We must lead gently like Paul. We must love with a Spirit-produced gentleness. The praise of Psalm 18:35 should be our declaration: "You have also given me the shield of Your salvation, and Your right hand upholds me; and Your gentleness makes me great" (NASB).

Ready to Receive

Think of the last several gatherings you have experienced. What primary characteristics would those you interacted with use to describe your communication with them? Would gentleness be near the top of the list? If not, how will you seek to apply the truths of this chapter?

Have you recently played the "my-day-can-beat-your-day game," even in a subtle way? Think of how our gentle Christ would interact in situations like this. Anticipate how you will submit to his mind and heart next time you are tempted to compete.

Reflect on Aesop's Fable about the wind versus the sun. Can you think of a relationship where you have been more like the wind? Prayerfully consider how you can begin to be the "sun" of the gentle "Son" next time you interact with this person. As gentleness produces a godly result, be sure to thank the Lord for the practical reality of his gospel wisdom.

Take time to experience the following Wisdom Prayer, allowing the biblical truths to renew your mind as your prayerful response draws your heart closer to Christ, who is your wisdom.

Wisdom Prayer

Strength Under Control

Peter wrote to persecuted and scattered Christians. He encouraged them to respond to unjust maltreatment in a way that honors God. Then he points them to the example of Jesus. This example will guide our prayers.

1 Peter 2:21–25

[21] For to this you have been called, because Christ also suffered for you,
leaving you an example, so that you might follow in his steps. [22] He
committed no sin, neither was deceit found in his mouth. [23] When he
was reviled, he did not revile in return; when he suffered, he did not
threaten, but continued entrusting himself to him who judges justly.
[24] He himself bore our sins in his body on the tree, that we might
die to sin and live to righteousness. By his wounds you have been
healed. [25] For you were straying like sheep, but have now returned to
the Shepherd and Overseer of your souls.

REVERENCE—"Who is God?"

Lord Jesus, I praise you because . . .

- You suffered willingly for us (v. 21)
- You are our example (v. 21)
- You empower us to walk in your steps (v. 21)
- You are sinless (v. 22)

- You were never deceitful (v. 22)
- You never retaliated in suffering (v. 23)
- You were a model of perfect trust (v. 23)
- You exalted God's justice (v. 23)
- You bore my sins at Calvary (v. 24)
- You empower us to die to sin and live to righteousness (v. 24)
- Your wounds have healed our lives (v. 24)
- You have become our Shepherd (v. 25)
- You are the Overseer of our souls (v. 25)

I praise you, Lord Jesus, that you are the ultimate example of ______________________. (v. 21)

I praise you that you were sinless and without deceit even when ______________________________. (v. 22)

I praise you, Father, that because you judge righteously (v. 23), I do not have to react, retaliate, or revile when ______________________________.

RESPONSE—"How should I respond?"

I confess that when I have felt dishonored and threatened I responded by ______________________________ rather than exhibiting trust in God, who judges righteously (v. 23). Give me a spirit of gentleness rather than competition and pride.

REQUESTS—"What should I pray about?"

Help me to walk in your steps, trusting the One who judges righteously, especially when ______________________________. (v. 23)

Because of your finished work on the cross, give me grace to die to sin and live to righteousness, especially in my dealings with ______________________________ [names]. (v. 24)

____________________ [name] needs the healing power of your gospel today (v. 24). Help me point them to you as I ____________________ [your plan to minister to them].

READINESS—"Where am I headed?"

As the world seeks to draw me away, help me not to stray toward ____________________ but to live in willing obedience to you, the Shepherd and Overseer of my soul. (v. 25)

REVERENCE—"Who is God?"

I praise you that as the Shepherd and Overseer of my soul, (v. 25) you are able to ____________________.

7

Wise Reason for Unreasonable People

The wisdom from above is . . . open to reason.

James 3:17

I find I am much prouder of the victory I obtain over myself, when, in the very ardor of dispute, I make myself submit to my adversary's force of reason, than I am pleased with the victory I obtain over him through his weakness.[1]

Michel de Montaigne

"You're being unreasonable!" This three-word exclamation, like a tornado siren in Kansas, is a warning—in this case, that a relationship is in trouble. It's a common response in many a disagreement, whether in marriage, work, or ministry. Sometimes the accused is indeed unable to see the flaw in his attitudes and arguments. Sometimes the accuser is upset that the other party refuses to agree with his or her own point of view. Most times, the wisdom from above that is "open to reason" has been neglected, sidelined, or outright rejected by both.

Wasteful Unreason

Years ago I was inserted in a dispute that had labored on for almost six years between a man who had been disciplined by his church and the elders, as they sought some kind of resolution. Incensed by the disciplinary action, he was suing the church for millions of dollars. As a wealthy man, he had the capacity to bankroll his own legal offense. The ordeal had been reported in the newspapers and consumed countless hours of negotiation. The parties were stuck in an impasse like an elephant in quicksand.

My first engagement was a multi-hour meeting at the man's home. Reminiscent of a championship game at Wimbledon, I watched as the elders and this man volleyed claims back and forth late into the evening. Prompting the end of the meeting, one of the elders stood up in a huff, threw his hands in the air, and walked out the door. He'd had enough. As he departed, he remarked that "emotions have no brains" and that the whole ordeal was a waste of time.

Without resolution, the lawsuit eventually expired under the statute of limitions. This prompted the fellow to write a scathing treatise, expounding on his many opinions and sundry accusations. He subsequently mailed this packet to hundreds of innocent bystanders, many of whom had no meaningful knowledge of the situation. This prompted the elders to make a clarifying statement about the original disciplinary action. Inflamed again, the man proceeded to *again* sue the church for scores of millions of dollars—twice the previous amount. This obviously made the news. In this new wave of angst, he leveled twelve counts against the church, eleven of which were thrown out by the judge. The final count was eventually resolved out of court by the church's insurance company. They settled for a few thousand dollars, but this antagonist had spent multiple thousands in legal fees, and God-only-knows how many hours consumed with this self-defense. God knows that throughout this process, all parties involved needed an understanding and empowerment of the wisdom from above that is "open to reason."

Reason's Suprising Relevance

Let's admit it: A breakdown of this gospel wisdom has led to global wars, national protests, community schisms, church splits, divided families, prodigal children, broken friendships, and unraveled marriages. Reason is not simply a function of logic, improved listening skills, or the pursuit of a general likeability. Reason comes from above, imparted by the all-wise God to the hearts of those who concede their needs, then trust in the abiding Christ to change their points of view and posturing in relating to others.

The Oxford Dictionary defines reason as "the power of the mind to think, understand, and form judgments by a process of logic." Biblically, reason certainly involves thinking, understanding, and judgment. Human logic may or may not be of help. The real source of biblical reason is the mind of Christ informing the thoughts and the Spirit of God ruling the will. As James uses it here, the meaning indicates the ability to yield to others without rancor or dispute or complaint. It includes being teachable, willing to change, and ready to forgive. The Greek word was used of a man who willingly submitted to military discipline, accepting and complying with whatever was demanded of him, and of a person who faithfully observes legal and moral standards.[2] Other versions describe this quality as being compliant, accommodating, submissive, and obedient. So on issues of absolute truth, this person is rock solid but gracious. On matters of relationship, this person is quick to yield, ready to forgive, and eager to comply. Only the wisdom of Christ helps us know the difference.

Society tells us that reason is the ability to win an argument. The New Testament emphasizes that reason is the ability to win by agreement. The first relies on outwitting the other person. The second delights in out-honoring the other person. The New Testament does not emphasize debates that lead to domination but a reasonableness that preserves the relationship and honors Christ. It is not attained by yelling but by yielding.

A Reasonable Example

Jesus is again our ultimate model. His submission to the Father and willingness to yield his rights in order to serve others inspires and empowers our obedience to this wisdom from above. The New Testament offers this explanation:

> Though he was God, he did not think of equality with God as something to cling to. Instead, he gave up his divine privileges; he took the humble position of a slave and was born as a human being. When he appeared in human form, he humbled himself in obedience to God and died a criminal's death on a cross.
>
> Philippians 2:6–8 NLT

As Michael Griffiths expresses,

> Here is one who lays aside the lifestyle and living standards of heaven to empty and humble himself in costly identification with human appearance, human nature and human experience. He leaves the sapphire-paved courts for a stable. He who holds the whole, wide world in his hands, allows himself to be carried as a helpless baby, unable to feed or clean himself. All human self-sacrifice pales into insignificance compared with the costly, suffering sacrifice of the incarnate Christ.[3]

So the inauguration of Jesus' incarnation was infused with the willingness to yield. His entire ministry was a model of a reasonable life as he gladly lived, not to be served but to serve and give himself for others. His final journey to the cross and sacrifice of his life for us heralded, "I am willing to yield." Again, we confirm, "He humbled himself by becoming obedient to the point of death, even death on a cross" (Philippians 2:8). Underscoring his willing sacrifice, Jesus said of his life, "No one takes it from me, but I lay it down of my own accord. I have authority to lay it down, and I have authority to take it up again" (John 10:18).

With this in mind, we must pray for the wisdom from above that gives us this very attitude when we would rather prove our point than point to him. Paul commanded it. Jesus supplies it. "Have this mind among yourselves, which is yours in Christ Jesus" (Philippians 2:5).

Not Like Jesus

The opposite of gospel reason is to be headstrong, obstinate, stubborn, quarrelsome, and rigid. I admit, after decades as a pastor, each of those descriptors bring to mind specific faces and names. I could even look in the mirror and wonder. I suspect you could too. I am sure your spouse could comment.

One of the sacred texts of Judaism is the *Pirqe Aboth*, a collection of sayings of the Jewish Fathers. In 5:17 it states, "There are four characters in dispositions. Easily provoked, and easily pacified, his gain is cancelled by his loss: hard to provoke and hard to pacify, his loss is cancelled by his gain: hard to provoke, and easily pacified, pious: easily provoked, and hard to pacify, wicked."[4] This quality identified by James is the third: a truly pious man. Proverbs states, "With those who take advice is wisdom" (13:10).

In our relationships we don't usually need more IQ but more WQ—wisdom quotient, found in the life of Christ. Reason is not always the result of the *acquisition* of biblical knowledge but rather the fruit of the *application* of biblical knowledge.

When I am reasonable, I am willing to listen to other points of view as if they were as valid as mine. I am able to dialogue with disagreeable people in a way that honors their perspectives. I am ready to accept a better idea when I realize the merit of its content. I am eager to support another direction when I understand its value and outcome. Writer William Barclay affirmed, "True wisdom is not rigid but is willing to listen and skilled in knowing when wisely to yield."[5]

Reasons for Reason

The early Christians needed a good share of this reasonable living. While we do not know all the details in each case, we know that conflicts surfaced in various churches. In Acts 6, there was a complaint about the unintentional neglect of the Greek-speaking widows in the Jerusalem church. In Acts 15, we read about a debate over the requirement of Jewish laws and how they applied to non-Jewish converts. Later in that chapter, the apostle Paul and Barnabas parted company because they did not see eye-to-eye in their views of John Mark, a young disciple who had been traveling with them. The congregation at Corinth had divided loyalties over the leaders in the church (1 Corinthians 1). In 1 Timothy 1:3–7, the apostle Paul called out some who were causing divisions, as he did in other letters (see Romans 16:17; 1 Corinthians 11:18; Titus 3:10–11; Jude 17–19).

One area of debate among the early Christians that required wisdom from above related to the legitimacy of enjoying a meal of discounted meat that had been offered to pagan idols earlier in the day. Some saw it as good stewardship and entirely permissible. Others were deeply troubled by the connection the meat had to idolatry. It seems a distant issue to us today, but the emotions ran hot and the debate had grown divisive. Paul had to intervene, as he wrote about in 1 Corinthians chapters 8–10, and in Romans chapter 14.

From these disputes they naturally passed judgment on one another. Their own legitimate "reasoning" had led to condemnation of those who held a different view. Paul advocated a transcendent kind of reason. Reasonableness infused with wisdom from above.

In Romans 14:10–12 he proposed,

> Why do you pass judgment on your brother? Or you, why do you despise your brother? For we will all stand before the judgment seat of God; for it is written, "As I live, says the Lord, every knee shall bow to me, and every tongue shall confess to God. So then each of us will give an account of himself to God."

The problem with judgment and a logical "winning argument" is that our primary motive can be to dominate others with our claims. Paul cuts to the quick and notes that, first of all, each side must recognize their ultimate accountability to God. We are accountable for how our "reasoning" has affected the other person and for our own emotions that drive the debate. Paul pulls the covers back on their attitudes, which he describes as "despising" the other party.

Similarly, James called out the readers for "bitter jealousy and selfish ambition" in their hearts (3:14). Then again, in James 4:1–3 he reveals that their fighting and quarrelling was driven by selfish passions. Like a sledgehammer on a nail, the New Testament drives home the point of every person's ultimate accountability to God for the issues of the heart that motivate unreasonable debates.

The Starting Point

Being "open to reason" starts with a life of submission and accountability to God. When you have a problem being reasonable, you have a problem with God.

Paul's correction of the quarreling Romans continues:

> Therefore let us not pass judgment on one another any longer, but rather decide never to put a stumbling block or hindrance in the way of a brother. I know and am persuaded in the Lord Jesus that nothing is unclean in itself, but it is unclean for anyone who thinks it unclean. For if your brother is grieved by what you eat, you are no longer walking in love. By what you eat, do not destroy the one for whom Christ died. So do not let what you regard as good be spoken of as evil.
>
> Romans 14:13–16

The heart behind New Testament reason is not to convince an opponent but rather to clear the way for the spiritual growth of others. Our reasoning must reflect a heart of genuine love for the other person. Otherwise, our determination to "make a good point" may produce a grievous effect that ultimately dishonors the heart of Christ. Paul reaffirmed this idea in these words: "'All things are lawful,' but not all things are helpful. 'All things are lawful,' but not all things build up. Let no one seek his own good, but the good of his neighbor" (1 Corinthians 10:23–24).

We must authentically embrace this teaching. Otherwise, we might win the logical contest but lose the spiritual war. We can win the argument but lose the relationship. We might win the battle but lose the Lord's blessing.

Paul tells us more about being open to reason:

> For the kingdom of God is not a matter of eating and drinking but of righteousness and peace and joy in the Holy Spirit. Whoever thus

> serves Christ is acceptable to God and approved by men. So then let us pursue what makes for peace and for mutual upbuilding.
>
> Romans 14:17–19

Sometimes the issue is not really the issue. What have you debated about lately with your wife, your children, a fellow believer—or even a non-Christian? What was the issue? But let me ask: Was that really the issue? Paul says the real issue should be an outcome of "righteousness, peace and joy in the Holy Spirit." Does our "reasoning" encourage right living, in an environment of peace, producing joy that only the Holy Spirit can generate? Proverbs 20:3 underscores this goal: "It is an honor for a man to keep aloof from strife, but every fool will be quarreling."

Let's see some final thoughts from Paul for the sake of our reasonableness:

> Do not, for the sake of food, destroy the work of God. Everything is indeed clean, but it is wrong for anyone to make another stumble by what he eats. It is good not to eat meat or drink wine or do anything that causes your brother to stumble.
>
> Romans 14:20–21

In summary, the goal of gospel reason is not to win the argument but to further the work of God in other people. My "position" is never to be used in a way that causes another to stumble, but rather to help them spiritually thrive. My goal is God's glory, not mine, in every engagement. As Paul testified, "So whether you eat or drink, or whatever you do, do all to the glory of God. Give no offense to Jews or to Greeks or to the church of God, just as I try to please everyone in everything I do, not seeking my own advantage, but that of many, that they may be saved" (1 Corinthians 10:31–33). The source of this reason is the gospel. The goal of this reason is also the gospel.

Absolutes vs. Negotiables

As you may have concluded, I am referring to issues that do not concern absolute truth. These might be matters of personal discretion, typically concerns not directly addressed in the Bible. This could include things allowed or disallowed, but outside the parameters of clear biblical orthodoxy.

We especially need to apply these guidelines for compliance to the most common disagreements that occur over non-biblical decisions in marriage and family. What house should we buy? What road should we take? What activities should we enjoy this weekend? This reasonableness must shape our dialogue with children who are trying to determine their boundaries, with spouses who are irritated with us, and with friends who just see the world through a different set of experiences.

But when it comes to the truth of the gospel, we must be clear and communicate without compromise. It is this truth that actually sets men free (John 8:31). This is the ultimate good for their souls. We must always urge others to abide in God's truth. Paul describes the attitude we must have as we do so: "Walk in wisdom toward outsiders, making the best use of the time. Let your speech always be gracious, seasoned with salt, so that you may know how you ought to answer each person" (Colossians 4:5–6).

Why So Unreasonable?

This sounds so good. So godly. But looking at our relational track records, we must confess our great need for a fresh empowerment of Christ-honoring wisdom. Why is reasonableness sometimes too elusive?

Ungodly Emotions

Headstrong, obstinate, stubborn, quarrelsome, and rigid relational interactions are often symptomatic of deeply held and unhealthy emotions. Paul identifies some of these attitudes in Ephesians 4:30–31: "And do not grieve the Holy Spirit of God, by whom you were sealed for the day of redemption. Let all bitterness and wrath and anger and clamor and slander be put away from you, along with all malice."

Old, unresolved hurts prevent us from a clear Godward trust and fuel our insecurities, suspicions, and competitions with other people.

Unaddressed, unrighteous anger is often the culprit. In one study many years ago, college students were asked to keep track of the things that made them angry. Eighty percent of the anger was a result of the actions of other people rather than circumstances or events.[6] As Jay Adams explains, when sinful anger (in contrast to righteous anger) is not resolved, it results in either internalization (clamming up) or ventilation (blowing up).[7] Clamming up results in "bitterness" and "malice." Blowing up can be seen in "clamor, slander," and "wrath."

It is easy to see why some people struggle to be reasonable, submissive, and willing to yield. Ungodly emotion negates wisdom's benefit. Proverbs 29:22 says, "A man of wrath stirs up strife, and one given to anger causes much transgression." James describes the proper response to the good gifts from the Father of Lights when he writes, "Let every person be quick to hear, slow to speak, slow to anger; for the anger of man does not produce the righteousness of God" (James 1:19–20). Anger coddled becomes bitterness. Hebrews 12:15 describes bitterness as a root. Roots don't go away—they go deeper and produce more fruit. In this case, fruit that defiles our relationships.

Returning to Ephesians 4, we can be reminded of Paul's words, "Be kind to one another, tenderhearted, forgiving one another, as God in Christ forgave you" (Ephesians 4:32). That's a great summary of reasonable behavior. Again it goes back to the gospel—the indwelling Christ who kindly and tenderheartedly provided forgiveness for us. If we will submit to him, we will also forgive and exhibit a fresh, reasonable grace in tense and troubled relationships.

Married couples can listen to one another with new ears and surrendered hearts. Disappointed church members can still support imperfect leaders. Frustrated employees can submit to a faithful God and respond in a Christ-honoring fashion when things seem unfair. They can even love their enemies and pray for those who persecute them because of the indwelling wisdom of Jesus (Matthew 5:44).

Needy and Controlling

Childhood traumas, past hurts, repeated comparisons, and various personal failures can often fuel inferiority, anxiety, competitiveness, and irrational reactions in our relationships. We become unreasonable as we react to conversations or relationships that seem to threaten us. Proverbs 18:2 describes it by saying, "A fool takes no pleasure in understanding, but only in expressing his opinion." Insecure, opinionated, defensive hearts struggle with reason.

Again, only the gospel can change this as we receive the healing grace of Christ's love and acceptance. We are free to submit to a trustworthy God and assume the best about others, even seeing them through eyes of trust and a secure eagerness to understand them, more than a need to be understood by them. One scholar describes the reasonable person of James 3:17 as "the person who gladly submits to true teaching and listens carefully for the other instead of attacking him."[8] The true teaching of our identity in Christ and the core security we have in him delivers us from attack mode.

Legalism's Rigidity

The most unreasonable characters in the New Testament were the most devout and religious. The Pharisees knew the Old Testament and expressed extreme devotion to the spiritual system of the day. Yet Jesus courageously and repeatedly confronted their unaccommodating rigidity. Their antagonisms ranged from a determination to stone a woman caught in adultery (John 8:1–11), their accusations of Jesus' disciples for failing to fast according their tradition (Mark 2:18–22; Luke 6:1–5), or their ire about Jesus' violation of the Sabbath in healing a man with a withered hand (Luke 6:6–10). Jesus did not mince his words in calling out their hypocrisy (more about this in chapter 12), but he passionately zeroed in on their legalism by saying, "Why do you break the commandment of God for the sake of your tradition?"(Matthew 15:3).

Legalism majors on the minors—the minor points of our extrabiblical rules, regulations, fixed biases, and rigid "convictions" about the way others should behave. Legalism is the creation of false standards of spirituality, then judging others by those standards. The fallout of legalism is the undermining of biblical love. Legalism often sacrifices relationships and the greater truths of authentic spirituality in the interests of safe, predictable, superficial rules of behavior. Reasonableness suffers. A legalist usually gets hardening of the attitudes before he gets hardening of the arteries.

Contrasting Stories

Our Henderson clan is notably a hotheaded bunch. I'd like to chalk it up to our type-A personalities or the fruit of growing up in a home of three competitive brothers. In honesty, it is a reflection of our need to pray and apply the wisdom from above.

On one occasion during my college years, I traveled on a ministry team, traversing the U.S., singing in churches and holding high school rallies. My brother, eleven years my senior, was the leader of that team. We loved the Lord, were gifted as preachers, and shared a mutual commitment to the ministry. But on one occasion, for reasons I do not even recall, we had a disagreement that was infused with Henderson hotheaded passion. For two weeks we did not speak to each other. Not one word, even though we were traveling and serving on the same team. Once we humbled ourselves and reconciled, we agreed that we needed divine help and grace to never go there again.

Contrast this with another incident that occurred when, as a young associate pastor, I was working for John MacArthur, a renowned Bible teacher and pastor from Southern California. One day his wife, Patricia, was conversing with a group of us young guys and made the staggering statement, "In all our years of marriage, I've never seen John lose his temper." We were baffled and tried to neutralize our guilt by joking, "That's because you don't play basketball with him."

The statement arrested me. So in a later conversation, I asked John to explain Pat's observation. He responded, "Well, it is my theology. You see, anger is a control mechanism, and I have such a high view of the sovereignty of God that, apart from some rare occasions of true righteous indignation, there's really not a lot that I have to get angry about." That proved to be a memorable and transformational conversation for me.

Like John, our reasonableness must be rooted in our high view of God, our personal submission to Christ, our love for reliable truth, and our Christ-centered desire to honor others. Starting with our faith in Christ's supremacy, his authority, his sure love, and his reasonable life, we can humbly yield to others in a practical demonstration of his wisdom.

I could not close this chapter without cherishing the reasonableness of God in Christ, seen in Isaiah 1:18–19:

> Come now, let us reason together, says the Lord: though your sins are like scarlet, they shall be as white as snow; though they are red like crimson, they shall become like wool. If you are willing and obedient, you shall eat the good of the land.

The gospel is a redemptive reasonableness. It leads to forgiveness, cleansing, goodness, spiritual health, and authentic relationships. That's why God loves to answer your prayer of faith, asking Christ to make you "open to reason" in your everyday relationships. It is a prayer that honors God's gospel purposes and shows the world a picture of our reasonable Savior.

Ready to Receive

If you were to ask your spouse or best friend if you are a "reasonable" person, what would they say and what examples would they give? If you then asked them how you could be more reasonable, what do you think they would suggest? Better yet, have this conversation and set your heart on a deeper experience of gospel wisdom.

Are your relationships ever hindered by your need to control? If so, what might be at the root of this tendency? Acknowledge these triggers and submit them regularly to the wisdom of a loving, grace-giving, and reasonable Christ. More specifically, think of an upcoming conversation or meeting and anticipate this empowerment in faith that he will give you the true wisdom you need.

Has a spirit of legalism ever undermined a relationship in your life? What have you learned about the wisdom of New Testament reason that can remedy and/or prevent this in the future? Ask Christ to rule your heart and mind in the future so that his wisdom can prevail.

Take time to experience the following Wisdom Prayer, allowing the biblical truths to renew your mind as your prayerful response draws your heart closer to Christ, who is your wisdom.

Wisdom Prayer

A Jesus-Kind of Reason

As we read in this chapter, Jesus Christ is the ultimate example of one who was reasonable, or willing to yield. This is powerfully communicated in Philippians 2:1–11, which will provide the basis for our prayers here.

Philippians 2:1–11

[1] So if there is any encouragement in Christ, any comfort from love,
any participation in the Spirit, any affection and sympathy, [2] complete
my joy by being of the same mind, having the same love, being in
full accord and of one mind. [3] Do nothing from selfish ambition or
conceit, but in humility count others more significant than yourselves.
[4] Let each of you look not only to his own interests, but also to the
interests of others. [5] Have this mind among yourselves, which is yours
in Christ Jesus, [6] who, though he was in the form of God, did not
count equality with God a thing to be grasped, [7] but emptied himself,
by taking the form of a servant, being born in the likeness of men. [8]
And being found in human form, he humbled himself by becoming
obedient to the point of death, even death on a cross. [9] Therefore
God has highly exalted him and bestowed on him the name that is
above every name, [10] so that at the name of Jesus every knee should

bow, in heaven and on earth and under the earth, [11] and every tongue confess that Jesus Christ is Lord, to the glory of God the Father.

REVERENCE—"Who is God?"

Lord Jesus, I praise you because . . .

- You are the source of encouragement (v. 1)
- You comfort us with your love (v. 1)
- You have brought us into participation with your Spirit (v. 1)
- You empower us to be of one mind, one in love, and in one accord (v. 2)
- You give us a humility that honors others (v. 3)
- You modeled what it meant to consider others (v. 4)
- You empower us to have your mind/attitude (v. 5)
- You willingly gave up the privileges of your eternal glory (v. 6)
- You came as a humble servant (v. 7)
- In humility you gave your very life on the cross (v. 8)
- You are exalted, bearing the name above every name (v. 9)
- At your name, every knee will someday bow (v. 10)
- Every tongue will confess that you are Lord (v. 10)
- Your life and work brings glory to God the Father (v. 11)

I praise you, Lord Jesus, that you were my source of encouragement when ______________________________. (v. 1)

I praise you that your love brought comfort to ___________________ when ______________________________. (v. 1)

I praise you because my experience of your Spirit has _______________ _______________ [benefits and blessings]. (v. 1)

RESPONSE—"How should I respond?"

I confess that I express rivalry and conceit (v. 3) in my relationships with ______________________________ [name]. Give me the grace of humility to pursue a oneness of mind and heart with them.

REQUESTS—"What should I pray about?"

Give me humility today to esteem ____________________ [names] as more significant than myself. (v. 3)

Help me to have your mind and to pay attention to the interests of others, above my own, when ________________. (v. 4)

Give me your grace to be like you as I "yield my rights" to ______________________________ [describe your common rights and expectations] in order to humbly serve others. (vv. 6–7)

READINESS—"Where am I headed?"

As the world entices me toward self-concern and self-protection, especially when ____________________, give me grace to walk in your steps of costly obedience. (v. 8)

REVERENCE—"Who is God?"

I praise you, Lord Jesus, that you are exalted and your name is above ____________________. (v. 9)

I praise you that someday even ______________________________ will confess that you are Lord, to the glory of God the Father. (v. 11)

8

Mercy Me, I'm Getting Wiser!

The wisdom from above is . . . full of mercy.

James 3:17

God loves to show mercy. He is not hesitant or indecisive or tentative in his desire to do good to his people his anger must be released by a stiff safety lock, but his mercy has a hair trigger.[1]

John Piper

There are few things more unsettling than looking in the rearview mirror to see a police car on your tail. As he follows, your thoughts explode with doubts like a Fourth of July fireworks show. *Was I speeding? Are my tags current? Are my brake lights working? Did I use my turn signal at that last corner? Did I come to a complete stop two blocks back?* We know law enforcement officers are ministers of justice, and when we are guilty we often must pay the price.

As believers, we are continuously followed, not by justice but by the God of mercy. Speaking of the sure, protecting, and comforting presence of God, David wrote, "Surely goodness and mercy shall follow me all the days of my life" (Psalm 23:6). John Piper describes this truth with these words: "God is like a highway patrolman pursuing you down the interstate with lights flashing and siren blaring to get you to stop—not to give you a ticket, but to give you a message so good it couldn't wait till you get home." I love that imagery.

I actually have a friend who has been stopped by law enforcement officers fifty-six times (as of this writing) and never received a ticket. Now that is mercy! (Actually, it is also due to my buddy's incredible people skills and gregarious and persuasive personality.)

We have all received similar and greater divine mercies in life, not because we have coerced God away from executing his justice, but because of his merciful character toward his children. And more specifically, because of the mercy we have received through the work of Jesus Christ.

Embracing the Mercy of Wisdom

When you pray for wisdom, expect to receive a full infusion and surprising expression of this necessary relational benefit. This is a prayer God loves to answer. But just what is this vital and biblically commended quality of mercy?

The Greek word *eleos* initially carried the idea of pity for a person who is suffering unjustly. The Christian idea of the word as it is used in the New Testament goes further. Scholar William Barclay explains,

> Christian pity is the reflection of God's pity; and that went out to men, not only when they were suffering unjustly, but when they were suffering through their own fault. We are apt to say of someone in trouble, "It is his own fault; he brought it on himself." And therefore, to feel no responsibility for him. Christian mercy is mercy for any man who is in trouble, even if he has brought that trouble on himself.[2]

As parents, this is easy to understand. As God requires in his dealings with us, we know that there will be consequences for disobedience. However, we also know that children do foolish things that bring harm and heartache. Our first reaction to our child getting hurt while playing on the playground is to rush to their aid, take them in our arms, comfort them in love, and assure them of our care. We would do a similar thing even with a child we did not know. The little guy may still have to get stitches and perhaps may even be restricted from the playground for a time, but mercy flows to them from natural parental love.

Our oldest son, growing up in a pastor's home, felt great pressure from church people to comply with superficial and sometimes legalistic expectations they imposed and carelessly communicated to him. Over time, he found acceptance instead with some less-than-stellar friends in high school. Over some very difficult and heartbreaking years we loved him, prayed for him, and did all we could to reclaim his heart. For several months we even put him in Los Angeles's The Dream Center—an intense, in-residence discipleship program. Unfortunately, his struggles continued until he encountered some significant legal trouble.

During the following months, we did not sit back and glibly declare, "You got what you deserved. You reap what you sow. We are tired of helping you." Never! We loved him, tried to understand, and did all we could to help him while still knowing there would be consequences. Justice did unfold but mercy prevailed. He went on to marry a beautiful Christian woman, finish his degree at a Christian college, complete his MBA, and is now working hard in a career and raising four beautiful children. Mercy has a beautiful, healing, helpful, and enduring power in our relationships.

Mercy has been described as anything we do for someone in need. It is unselfish compassion. Love sustains and multiplies the blessing of mercy to others. Mercy is often confused with grace. Grace and mercy are different but catalytic in their benefit. Mercy is God withholding from us what we rightly deserve. Grace is God abundantly lavishing us with favor we do not deserve. Grace drew us to the cross. Mercy appropriated the blessing of the cross to our lives. Grace empowers us to live a life worthy of the cross. Grace and mercy will carry us until the day we see the One who gave his life for us on that cross.

God of Mercy!

God's mercies are abundant and observed everywhere. Pastor Charles J. Rolls gave this wonderful description:

> The mercies of the Lord are demonstrated throughout the entire creation, for all of which we are indebted to the excellence of his transcendent nature of wisdom. We may mention some of these: the fragrance of the flowers, the beauty of birds, the foliage of the forest, the majesty of mountains, the fruits of the field, the flavors of food, the shining of sunlight, the splendor of sunsets, the scintillation of stars, the succession of seasons, the refreshment of rains, the distilling of dews, the melodies of music, and a thousand more, express the amazing riches of wisdom's mercies. In addition and in greater volume are the blessing of wisdom which are too numerous to mention all of which emanate from Christ Jesus the Lord.[3]

When we pray for wisdom from above, God, who rules in the heavens and regards the estate of his children, gladly provides abundant mercy through Christ. How merciful is God? In the Scriptures, he has given us overwhelming cause to worship the wisdom of his mercy.

Psalm 136:1 declares, "Oh, give thanks to the Lord: for He is good! For His mercy endures forever" (NKJV). In this Psalm, praise for his mercy (also translated "steadfast love") repeatedly resounds in every one of the twenty-six verses. The Bible tells us his mercy is "abounding" (Psalm 86:5), "tender" (Luke 1:78), and "great" (1 Peter 1:3); we often speak and sing of his great mercy. "The steadfast love of the Lord never ceases; his mercies never come to an end; they are new every morning; great is your faithfulness" (Lamentations 3:22–23).

A. W. Pink explains more:

> The mercy of God has its spring in the Divine goodness. The first issue of God's goodness is his benignity or bounty, by which he gives liberally to his creatures as creatures; thus has he given being and life to all things. The second issue of God's goodness is his mercy, which denotes the ready inclination of God to relieve the misery of fallen creatures. Thus, "mercy" presupposes sin.[4]

We will look at the power and experience of God's goodness in the next chapter but, at this moment, we must reiterate that it is our sin that makes his mercy so magnificent. Puritan writer Thomas Goodwin noted, "It is the highest subject, the richest text, and the most renowned description of the nature of God. The Lord God, merciful and gracious, slow to anger, and abounding in lovingkindness."[5]

Christ of Mercy!

Whenever a broken soul cried out to Jesus, "Have mercy on me!"—he did. Jesus knew better than any the devastating consequences of sin and the struggle of the human soul. "[Jesus] himself knew what was in man" (John 2:25). Hebrews 4:15 assures us that Jesus was "tempted as we are" and able to "sympathize with our weaknesses." His life was a life of continuous, compassionate mercy. Study the miracles of Jesus and each will be stamped with an unquestionable endorsement of magnanimous mercy!

The gospels provide some samplings of his indescribable and profound mercy. We see him forgiving a woman caught in adultery, giving sight to the blind, restoring health to the lepers, raising the dead to life, compassionately feeding thousands who had no food, delivering the oppressed from demon possession, sharing meals with despised tax collectors and sinners, calming a storm on the Galilean lake, generously providing a catch for hungry and weary fishermen-disciples, restoring the severed ear of a Roman soldier, offering hope to a guilty thief on a cross, and graciously restoring a cowardly Peter to a place of spiritual usefulness.

All of these moments were subthemes to the greatest mercy we find in Christ. Christ, the sinless, divine Son of God, was perfect. Yet God's holiness demanded a satisfaction of his just wrath against our sin. Judgment demanded atonement for sin. Mercy made it possible. As author Tim Challies describes,

> Christ walked into that courtroom, stood between the judge and the guilty person, and said, "I will serve his sentence." He took other people's sin upon himself. He took upon himself sin to such an extent that he became sin. He became vile and detestable in God's eyes—the most vile and detestable thing that could ever exist—and God poured out the full measure of his wrath upon him. He poured out his wrath upon Christ until that wrath was absorbed and exhausted, until every bit of justice was satisfied. Christ served the complete sentence of just

wrath that I deserved. This is the mercy of the cross, the sinless one serving the sentence of the sinner.[6]

Mercy had a steep price tag, and Jesus paid it all on the cross. I've often noted that there was only one time in all of history where God was unfair. The Father was merciless on the innocent Christ so that he could pour out his mercy on those who are guilty. The writer of Hebrews nails it when he says, "Therefore he had to be made like his brothers in every respect, so that he might become a merciful and faithful high priest in the service of God, to make propitiation for the sins of the people" (Hebrews 2:17).

The Bible describes God's mercy to us in Christ so prolifically that we cannot help but exclaim, "Blessed be the God and Father of our Lord Jesus Christ!" Why? Because "according to his great mercy, he has caused us to be born again to a living hope through the resurrection of Jesus Christ from the dead" (1 Peter 1:3). We worship him as "the Father of mercies and God of all comfort" (2 Corinthians 1:3). We praise him as our God who "being rich in mercy, because of the great love with which he loved us, even when we were dead in our trespasses, made us alive together with Christ—by grace you have been saved" (Ephesians 2:4–5). Hallelujah! "He saved us, not because of works done by us in righteousness, but according to his own mercy, by the washing of regeneration and renewal of the Holy Spirit" (Titus 3:5). He did all this "in order to make known the riches of his glory for vessels of mercy, which he has prepared beforehand for glory" (Romans 9:23). We are now recipients and agents of this amazing mercy from above all found in the treasures of Christ.

Subterranean vs. Supernatural Mercy

Mercy is noted as a spiritual gift (Romans 12:8). This means that some believers are especially graced, not just to show mercy but to conduct and even lead ministries that exhibit extraordinary mercy. They actually enjoy and do it with great cheerfulness. These might be endeavors like a homeless shelter, a food bank, outreach to the incarcerated, or local and international initiatives that focus on the poor and disenfranchised.

Honestly, that is not my spiritual gift. My assessments and experiences have shown that my primary gifts are teaching, leadership, and faith. I have often confessed that my "mercy" gift is subterranean.

Yet there is a supernatural enabling that God gives each of us as the recipients of his mercy. I can testify that on countless occasions Christ in me has manifested mercy. I have felt it in my marriage, my parenting, my counseling, and my preaching. Mercy has overwhelmed me as I have led prayer events where men sat sobbing and broken, confessing their sins and seeking restoration with the Lord, their wives, and their families. "Weeping with those who weep" has been a beautiful taste of wisdom's mercy.

I will never forget the night I received a call from a distraught wife. I had counseled her and her husband numerous times as they sought help after years of trouble in their marriage. She had learned that one of her husband's college girlfriends had come to town, and he went to meet her at a hotel room in the area. I quickly wrote a letter to the husband, confronting his sin, appealing to his repentance, and calling him back to Christ and his wife. Within the hour I was in the hotel lobby, calling his room, asking him to join me there. He read my letter as I watched and waited. He began to weep with tears of humility and repentance. After some direct and heartfelt conversation, we went together to the hotel room, spoke to the girlfriend, and packed his bags. I prayed with them, asking for a triumph of truth, holiness, and restoration in this situation. I followed the husband's car as he left the hotel premises to head home to his wife and family. Humanly, I had felt like strangling the guy. But at that moment, I had a new sense of the mercy of God that shines brightest against a backdrop of sin and failure but always leads to restoration and hope.

Mercy Balances Justice

Mercy does not cancel justice, but it does balance it. Justice is necessary for the upholding of both moral and civil law to ensure societal well-being. Justice is a deterrent to unchecked crime and moral decadence in civilization. It's been said that everyone wants justice until it applies to them, and then they want mercy. Biblically, justice is necessary to glorify the holiness, truth, and righteousness of God.

When Judah was rebelling against God and seeking ungodly alliances with pagan Egypt, God gave a generous appeal: "For thus said the Lord God, the Holy One of Israel, 'In returning and rest you shall be saved; in quietness and in trust shall be your strength.' But you were unwilling" (Isaiah 30:15). He then assures them of their judgment and demise. Their rebellion required chastisement—but for the purpose of repentance, restoration, and the renown of his holy name. Then we find this incredible promise that immediately follows: "Therefore the Lord waits to be gracious to you, and therefore he exalts himself to show mercy to you. For the Lord is a God of justice; blessed are all those who wait for him" (Isaiah 30:18).

In our lives, God metes justice as necessary for our good and his glory. Yet he longs to be gracious. He purposes to exalt himself by the pouring out of his mercy. He waits to bless and make happy those who will wait on him.

Mercy gloriously honors God's holiness but ultimately points to the work of Christ. When mercy reflects the substitutionary sacrifice and merciful character of Christ, it then adorns the gospel, affects a broken soul, softens a hard heart, transforms a lost sinner, and displays the riches of God's gospel wisdom. It becomes an essential expression of authentic Christianity.

Mercy Exalts Christ

At the outset of his ministry, Jesus set the stage for a profound lavishing of mercy on those in need. Returning to his hometown of Nazareth, following his baptism and temptation in the wilderness, he entered the synagogue and read from the Old Testament scroll. As one writer has commented, "The essential purpose of God in Christ can be seen in this manifesto. . . . This is the text, therefore, upon which the sermon of Jesus' life and ministry develops."[7] Here is the account:

> And the scroll of the prophet Isaiah was given to him. he unrolled the scroll and found the place where it was written,

> "The Spirit of the Lord is upon me, because he has anointed me to proclaim good news to the poor. He has sent me to proclaim liberty to the captives and recovering of sight to the blind, to set at liberty those who are oppressed, to proclaim the year of the Lord's favor."
>
> And he rolled up the scroll and gave it back to the attendant and sat down. And the eyes of all in the synagogue were fixed on him. And he began to say to them, "Today this Scripture has been fulfilled in your hearing."
>
> Luke 4:17–21

Did you notice the passion and purview of his heart? The poor, the captives, the blind, the oppressed—all in need of good news, liberty, recovery, and favor. This initial mission announcement that magnifies mercy is so distant from the opening lines of much of today's ministry. We "launch" with ad campaigns, social media blitzes, target-grouped promotions, and slick images of a high-powered pastor and pictures of happy people purchased on iStock. What might it really mean for us to embrace the wisdom from above that is full of mercy as the starting place of all ministry? This could radically honor the Savior, whose name we proclaim and footsteps we follow.

Curiosity and Threat

It is hard for us to conceive of the sweeping nature of the message of Christ when he described his kingdom and the essential virtues of his devoted followers. When he preached, "Blessed are the merciful, for they shall receive mercy" (Matthew 5:7), it was like a jolt of bewilderment to Roman society. As Jesus lived a life of extravagant, miraculous mercy, it certainly evoked curiosity and even posed a threat to some.

Roman philosophers viewed mercy as the disease of the soul. To them, mercy was an indication of weakness. The Romans glorified justice, discipline, authority, and power. As an example, the Roman father had the right of *patria potestas* over his children. They would hold the child up and if he wanted the child to live, he gave thumbs-up. If for any reason he wanted the child to die, it was thumbs-down. At the father's displeasure, the child was immediately drowned. Similarly, if a Roman citizen was unhappy with his slave, he could kill the slave at will. This was the merciless authority and twisted justice of the day. In some ways, our day is not much different. Mercy is not always valued in politics, communities, work environments—even churches, friendships, and families. This is why mercy exalts Christ so gloriously. Only Christ, the treasure of wisdom and knowledge, can change a life with the power of divine mercy.

When Jesus declared that his followers would be blessed and happy, due to their experience and expressions of mercy, it sounded like a foreign language. As John MacArthur explains, Jesus essentially proclaimed,

> The people in my kingdom aren't takers, they're givers. The people in my kingdom aren't condemners, they're mercy givers. The people in my kingdom aren't the ones who set themselves above everybody, they're the people who stoop to help everybody. . . . [They] actually get in the skin of another person, to actually get right in and think their thoughts and feel their emotions and then care for them in a very tangible way.[8]

This is the wisdom from above, given generously to those who ask in faith. God loves to arrest our hearts, conquer our carnality, and parade his power by lavishing us with his mercy for the sake of others.

At the Cross

Several years ago I was co-leading a regional prayer summit that involved pastors and seminary students in a multi-day gathering of what I describe as Scripture-fed, Spirit-led, worship-based prayer. This environment features no formal agenda but is driven by Scripture readings, songs, and prayers offered in a free-flowing format by the participants.

As we typically do, we devoted one entire evening to a focus on the cross and saving work of Christ, leading to an extended communion experience. On this night, one of my associates was actually leading the session, which gave me more freedom to embrace and cherish the experience without the distraction of facilitating.

Toward the end of the evening we sang some of the great old hymns. Two lines from these songs captivated my heart that night: "Mercy there was great and grace was free. Pardon there was multiplied to me. There my burdened soul found liberty—at Calvary."[9] Then came another cherished chorus: "At the cross, at the cross, where I first saw the light and the burden of my heart rolled away. It was there by faith I received my sight and now I am happy all the day."[10]

My associate asked us to respond by expressing our gratitude for the mercy of God. We were urged to specifically thank him for the personal burdens that were "rolled away" because of our salvation through the work of Christ on the cross.

I was overwhelmed to the point of significant, prolonged tears of gratitude. You see, I was not born into a Christian home, but I was raised in one. When I was one year old, my entire family was powerfully transformed by the gospel.

Ours was a military family. My dad was a U.S. Air Force pilot. My parents were lost in destructive spiritual darkness. Before my birth their marriage was devastated by extramarital affairs, divorce, remarriage (to each other), alcoholism, and abuse. My older brothers, fourteen and eleven years my senior, remember nights of violent arguing, other men sleeping over, and months on end when Dad was absent.

All I remember from my formative years was a family that was radically redeemed. My parents were at church, perhaps more than any family—serving with joy. They led associates, relatives, and neighbors to Christ. I was truly "mercied" by the cross. The burden of my heart—a broken, dysfunctional, and sin-devastated family—was rolled away when I was just one year old. Certainly underserving and even unaware, I experienced the mercy of God in Christ that changed everything.

I can never forget the mercy of Christ to my family and, accordingly, to my life. Of course, I came to a personal saving experience of that mercy some years later (providentially under the preaching of my brother, who went on to become a pastor). Oh, what great mercy!

Full of Mercy

That's my mercy story. What's yours? What burdens of your heart were rolled away at Calvary? Mercy there was great and grace was free—for you. For your unique story. For his glory. To make you a grateful and transformed recipient of his wisdom—so that his wisdom will flow through you as you are *full* of mercy.

This is your promise and God's delight. So when you are tempted to be short-tempered or unsympathetic toward your spouse, ask God to fill you with mercy. When someone fails and falters and you are irritated or inconvenienced—call on God. By the way, to be "full" of mercy implies being *controlled* by mercy. He can dominate you with beautiful mercy. In a cruel and unforgiving world, you can shine as a beacon because you are truly full and overflowing with mercy.

The Jesus Prayer

In many orthodox churches they practice "The Jesus Prayer." This is a short prayer that simply says, "Lord Jesus Christ, Son of God, have mercy on me, a sinner." It is repeated very often in corporate services and personally—and is understood as the introductory words to a life of praying without ceasing.

Orthodox scholars emphasize that the Greek word for *mercy* has the same root as the word for *olive* or *olive tree*, including the oil from it. They often point to the early picture of the olive tree in Genesis when, after the flood, a dove released by Noah brought back the small branch of an olive tree. This twig conveyed the news that the wrath of God had ceased and that God was now offering humankind a fresh opportunity. All those who were in the ark would have a new beginning on firm ground.

These scholars also note that in the parable of the Good Samaritan, olive oil is poured to soothe and to heal, as was a common usage in biblical times. They further note the use of olive oil in the anointing of kings and priests in the Old Testament as a symbol of blessing, power, and grace.

One writer notes, "The oil speaks first of all of the end of the wrath of God, of the peace which God offers to the people who have offended against him; further it speaks of God healing us in order that we should be able to live and become what we are called to be."[11]

May the oil of God's mercy continue to be poured upon us, working in us and flowing through us to bring healing and blessing to those we love and will be called to love. This mercy produces an amazing array of goodness in this world—and your world—your home, your workplace, your church, your community. As a result, you will be full of true and abounding goodness. That's the next prayer God loves to answer.

Ready to Receive

Picture the mercy of God in constant and passionate pursuit, following you all the days of your life. If this picture became the default reality of your thinking, how might your experience and example of mercy toward others be different tomorrow?

Do you consider mercy as one of your spiritual gifts? If so, how is it evident and how can the truths of the chapter strengthen your ministry? If not, consider the many opportunities you will have to invite the wisdom of a merciful Jesus to supersede your natural personality. Think of just one such opportunity that might arise in the next few days and set your heart to submit to Christ that you might demonstrate real gospel wisdom.

Like the story told in this chapter, consider the mercy of the cross and the burdens of your heart that have been rolled away as a result. Name them as they come to mind. Now, think of a few "burdened" people in your life. Imagine how the wise mercy of Jesus expressed through you might bless them. Plan to turn that imagination into reality in the next few days.

Take time to experience the following Wisdom Prayer, allowing the biblical truths to renew your mind as your prayerful response draws your heart closer to Christ, who is your wisdom.

Wisdom Prayer

Wonderful, Merciful Savior

One of the early and bold announcements from Jesus about his identity and ministry came in Luke 4:16–21. He stood in the synagogue at Nazareth reading from Isaiah 61:1–2. He actually stopped reading from Isaiah prior to the end of verse 2, which referenced God's vengeance. Clearly Jesus was announcing himself as Messiah and indicating the nature of his merciful and gracious ministry. This text will guide our prayers.

Luke 4:16–21

16 And he came to Nazareth, where he had been brought up. And as
was his custom, he went to the synagogue on the Sabbath day, and he
stood up to read. 17 And the scroll of the prophet Isaiah was given to
him. He unrolled the scroll and found the place where it was written,
18 "The Spirit of the Lord is upon me, because he has anointed me to
proclaim good news to the poor. He has sent me to proclaim liberty
to the captives and recovering of sight to the blind, to set at liberty
those who are oppressed, 19 to proclaim the year of the Lord's favor."
20 And he rolled up the scroll and gave it back to the attendant and
sat down. And the eyes of all in the synagogue were fixed on him. 21
And he began to say to them, "Today this Scripture has been fulfilled
in your hearing."

REVERENCE—"Who is God?"

Lord Jesus, I praise you because . . .

- You were the anointed one—Messiah (v. 18)
- You have brought the world the Good News of the gospel (v. 18)
- You have brought good news to the poor (v. 18)
- You have delivered liberty to the captives (v. 18)
- You have given sight to the blind (v. 18)

- You have brought liberty to the oppressed (v. 18)
- You have provided God's favor to man (v. 19)
- You are the fulfillment of the prophecies of the Old Testament about the Messiah (v. 21)

I praise you, Lord Jesus, that you revealed the Good News of the gospel to me when I was ______________________ [your spiritual condition before Christ]. (v. 18)

I praise you that you have set me free from ______________________ ________. (v. 18)

RESPONSE—"How should I respond?"

I confess that many days I encounter people who are ____________ ________________, and I fail to announce your Good News to them (v. 18). Open my heart to their needs and my mouth to share the favor of your gospel.

REQUESTS—"What should I pray about?"

Give me a heart of mercy to bring your Good News to the poor (v. 18) as I ______________________________ [describe a ministry context you can pursue].

Give me a heart of mercy to share the freedom of your life to those who are held captive and oppressed (v. 18) by ________________ ______________.

Give me a heart of mercy toward ________________________ [name], who is spiritually blind (v. 18) and in need of the light of the gospel.

READINESS—"Where am I headed?"

As I enter a world of brokenness and doubt, give me confidence that the Spirit of God is also with me (v. 18) to proclaim your truth even when ___________________________.

REVERENCE—"Who is God?"

I praise you that you fulfilled the promises of the Old Testament in your first coming and will fulfill your promises when you come again. I am confident that you will ____________________.

9

How the Good Die Wise

The wisdom from above is . . . full of . . . good fruits.
James 3:17

Do all the good you can,
By all the means you can,
In all the ways you can,
In all the places you can,
At all the times you can,
To all the people you can,
As long as ever you can.[1]
John Wesley

In the next few days, tune in to the common expression of the word *good* as it is used in conversations, news stories, and modern-day culture. In all likelihood, you will hear references like:

- "It's all good!"
- "That was a good movie."
- "She's a good woman."
- "The weather looks good."

- "Good game, son!"
- "He's good-looking."
- "The food was good."
- "It's good that you were here."
- "He's a good preacher."
- "I feel good about it."
- "Sounds good."
- "Good Lord!"
- "That was a good crowd."
- "This will be good for you."
- "They had a good selection."
- "Oh my goodness!"

Of course, the interpretation of these few phrases can yield a convoluted and even confusing understanding of goodness. Just to prove the point, look over each phrase and try to figure exactly what is meant by the word *good*. These common expressions (and there are *many* others) remind us of the subjective nature of the word.

So when we read a verse like Galatians 6:10, which says, "As we have opportunity, let us do good to everyone, and especially to those who are of the household of faith," what does this "good" look like?

The Reader's Digest Complete Oxford Word Finder devotes a full page of very fine print to various definitions of *good*. Plato taught that *good* was the power that preserves and supports in contrast to evil, which spoils and destroys. Aristotle taught that the goal of all action was the attainment of something good. In general, the idea of good or goodness refers to a desirable quality, something commendable, reliable, welcome, enjoyable, beneficent, kind, noble, admirable, or exemplary. "Goodness" usually speaks of the inner qualities of virtue, also an excellent character, morality, and attitude.

So as we ask God above for the wisdom that is full of good fruits, we can ask in faith, but we probably need some clarification to better understand the source, nature, and result of these good fruits. Especially as we trust God above to give us this quality through Christ and for the sake of our relationships.

Ultimate Goodness

Jesus stated, "No one is good except God alone" (Mark 10:18). We know that no one is righteous—not even one—and all have sinned (Romans 3:10, 23). Ultimately, only God is absolutely good and the source of all good.

A. W. Pink explains that the goodness of God refers to the perfection of his nature and that nothing is lacking in it or defective in it, and nothing can be added to it to make it better.[2] Puritan writer Thomas Manton states,

> He is originally good, good of himself, which nothing else is; for all creatures are good only by participation and communication from God. He is essentially good; not only good, but goodness itself; the creature's goodness is but a drop, but in God there is an infinite ocean and sea, or gathering together of goodness.[3]

The Bible encourages us to consider the goodness of God (Romans 11:22). Psalm 119:68 declares, "You are good and do good." God has "laid up" goodness for those who trust him (Psalm 31:19 NKJV). Psalm 52:1 says "the goodness of God endures continually." It is as eternal as God is and will never stop. God crowns our years with goodness (Psalm 65:11 NKJV) and fills our journey with so much blessing. Beyond the tangible provisions of life, "God fills the hungry soul with goodness" (Psalm 107:9 NKJV).

Certainly, bad things happen in all of our lives. We suffer losses, go through disappointments, experience failures, and endure hurts. However, God's abundant, constant, and sometimes imperceptible goodness transcends it all. Our responsibility is to trust him even when we don't see the way, follow him even when we don't know the way, and seek him until he shows us the way. We do this with the firm conviction that he is absolutely, reliably good. And he produces his goodness in and through us for his glory.

Charles Spurgeon observed,

> When others behave badly to us, it should only stir us up the more heartily to give thanks unto the Lord because he is good; and when we ourselves are conscious that we are far from being good, we should only

> the more reverently bless him that "he is good." We must never tolerate an instant's unbelief as to the goodness of the Lord; whatever else may be questionable, this is absolutely certain, that Jehovah is good; his dispensations may vary, but his nature is always the same, and always good. It is not only that he was good, and will be good, but he is good; let his providence be what it may. Therefore let us even at this present moment, though the skies be dark with clouds, yet give thanks unto his name.[4]

Nancy DeMoss Wolgemuth affirms, "[God] is good whether or not His choices seem right to us, whether or not we feel it, whether or not it seems true, and whether or not He gives us everything that we want."[5]

Whatever our perceptions of our circumstances in life, we can anchor our souls in knowing "the Lord God is a sun and shield; the Lord bestows favor and honor. No good thing does he withhold from those who walk uprightly" (Psalm 84:11).

Good From the Start

From the beginning, God displayed his goodness: "And God saw everything that he had made, and behold, it was very good. And there was evening and there was morning, the sixth day" (Genesis 1:31). The story of creation confirms the "earth is full of the goodness of the Lord" (Psalm 33:5 NKJV). He did not have to make the stars to strike wonder in our hearts, a sun to warm us, a moon to light the night, colors to delight the eyes, food to satisfy with countless flavors, aromas to please us, our sense of feeling to excite us, the sound of birds and ocean shores to delight us (or hundreds of other indications of his goodness)—but he did. The earth proclaims his goodness.

His dealings with mankind have been good. "Oh, that *men* would give thanks to the Lord *for* his goodness, And *for* his wonderful works to the children of men! For he satisfies the longing soul, and fills the hungry soul with goodness" (Psalm 107:8–9). Speaking of life's basic blessings of marriage and food, Paul writes to Timothy, "For every creature of God *is* good, and nothing is to be refused if it is received with thanksgiving" (1 Timothy 4:4 NKJV).

The ultimate manifestation of goodness came in Christ. At his birth, the angels announced, "Glory to God in the highest and on earth peace, goodwill toward men!" (Luke 2:14). All the fullness of the Godhead was evident and expressed in Christ (Colossians 2:9). He is holy goodness in the flesh, truly full of good fruits.

God's Good Work in Us

Michelangelo was once asked what he was doing as he chipped away at a shapeless rock. He replied, "I'm liberating an angel from this stone." God is liberating agents of goodness from an old life of sin to a new life of meaning through the work of Christ. Ephesians 2:10 offers a clear purpose for God saving us and leaving us here on earth: "For we are his workmanship, created in Christ Jesus for good works, which God prepared beforehand, that we should walk in them." As you've likely heard, the Greek word for "workmanship" is *poiema*, from which we get our English words *poem* and *poetry*. We are a creative masterpiece whose mission is to live out the good works God has determined for our earthly journey.

Pastor Timothy Keller elaborates,

> Do you know what it means that you are God's workmanship? What is art? Art is beautiful, art is valuable, and art is an expression of the inner being of the maker, of the artist. Imagine what that means. You're beautiful, you're valuable, and you're an expression of the very inner being of the Artist, the divine Artist, God himself. You see, when Jesus gave himself on the Cross, he didn't say, "I'm going to die just so you know I love you." He said, "I'm going to die, I'm going to bleed, for your splendor. I'm going to re-create you into something beautiful. I will turn you into something splendid, magnificent. I'm the Artist; you're the art. I'm the Painter; you're the canvas. I'm the Sculptor; you're the marble. You don't look like much there in the quarry, but I can see. Oh, I can see!" Jesus is an Artist! And you beloved are his crowning achievement, his masterpiece![6]

Paul prayed that we would meet that destiny as he wrote with longing that we would bear fruit in every good work as we are increasing in the knowledge of God (Colossians 1:10).

When we know a good God, love a good Christ, are indwelt by his good Spirit, we can pray in confidence for a fullness of good fruit in our lives. It is a prayer God loves to answer because he has destined this as our lifestyle.

Goodness Inhibitors

Still, many who claim to follow Christ seem distant from the reality of his goodness, both in feeling the embrace of a good God and in being able to express his goodness to others. In his book *The Pleasures of God*, John Piper proposes four goodness-robbing culprits: guilt over great personal sin, people who instigate and wish bad upon us, feeling small and far away from the greatness of God, and feelings of defeat and shame from people who always put us down.[7] We have all felt these things at some point in our journey.

I would testify that the experience of goodness is very *daily*. In my book *The Deeper Life: Satisfying the 8 Vital Longings of the Soul*,[8] I teach on the daily renewal process that has powerfully sustained me for twenty years as I have regularly renewed my mind in biblical truths about my theology, my identity, and my purpose. These principles have helped me experience a daily "WIN" (through Worship, Integrity, and Non-Conformity to the world). At the core of this renewal process has been the truth of God's absolute goodness,[9] my identity as one created for good works,[10] and my good and meaningful purpose in this life. We can overcome the goodness-robbers each day by being transformed through the renewing of our mind, thus avoiding conformity to the world's antagonism and attacks on God's goodness.

The great missionary statesman Oswald Chambers said, "The root of all sin is the suspicion that God is not good." Our ancestors in the Garden of Eden exemplify this. The serpent called into question the goodness of God's plan and command for Adam and Eve, leading to the fall. Nothing has changed. One of our enemy's primary tactics is to incite us to doubt the absolute goodness of God and his ways. All sorts of negative feelings and sinful attitudes naturally follow.

Romans 2:4 notes that at the core of a life that rejects God is the act of despising "the riches of his goodness." On the other hand, a serious understanding and embrace of God's goodness actually leads us to repentance. His goodness compels us to draw near, get right, and live well in light of his truthfulness, trustworthiness, tenderness, long-suffering, kindness, mercy, love, and grace that are all summed up in the attribute of his goodness.

The Mercy + Goodness Connection

James links "mercy and good fruits" just as Psalm 23 connects them: "Goodness and mercy shall follow me all the days of my life" (Psalm 23:6). Four times in Psalm 107 we are told to give thanks to the Lord for his goodness and his wonderful works in our lives (v. 8, 15, 21, 31). In Psalm 118:1, we also read, "Oh, give thanks to the Lord, for he *is* good! For his mercy *endures* forever" (NKJV).

Psalm 136:25 speaks of God's practical goodness, stemming from his mercy: "He gives food to all flesh, for his mercy *endures* forever" (NKJV). When we are recipients of the great mercy of God in Christ, it follows that we will be full of good fruits.

Charles Spurgeon taught:

> Mercy is a great part of his goodness, and one which more concerns us than any other, for we are sinners and have need of his mercy. Angels may say that he is good, but they need not his mercy and cannot therefore take an equal delight in it; inanimate creation declares that *he is good*, but it cannot feel his *mercy*, for it has never transgressed; but man, deeply guilty and graciously forgiven, beholds mercy as the very focus and center of the goodness of the Lord. The endurance of the divine mercy is a special subject for song: notwithstanding our sins, our trials, our fears, his mercy *endureth forever*. The best of earthly joys pass away, and even the world itself grows old and hastens to decay, but there is no change in the mercy of God.[11]

Mercy + Goodness = Transforming Wisdom

God loves to answer our prayers for a fullness of mercy and good fruit, and does so most effectively when we hunger for his Word. Through his good truth we experience the fullness of this wisdom, which is truth applied to life. "Your rules are good" (Psalm 119:39). A good God gives us his good word, "You are good and do good; teach me your statutes" (Psalm 119:68). Nehemiah exalted God's "good statutes and commandments" (9:13), and Hebrews 6:5 describes Christians as those who "have tasted the goodness of the word of God." His inspired Word is profitable to equip us for "every good work" (2 Timothy 3:16–17). As we are "transformed by the renewing of our mind," we "discern what is the will of God, what is good and acceptable and perfect" (Romans 12:2).

Mercy + Goodness = Trust

Because we know such great mercy from a good God, we can exhibit the fruit of trust. Elisabeth Elliot stated it well: "God never withholds from His child that which His love and wisdom call good. God's refusals are always merciful—'severe mercies' at times, but mercies all the same. God never denies us our hearts' desire except to give us something better."[12]

Perhaps you've read of George Mueller, a man of great faith and prayer who lived in Bristol, England, in the 1800s. Through his orphanages he cared for over 10,000 children, and the schools he established educated over 120,000 students. But he faced serious tests to his faith in the goodness of God. One occurred when the Muellers' only child, Lydia, almost died of typhoid fever in 1853. Seventeen years later, George's wife, Mary, died of rheumatic fever. They had been married for over thirty-nine years. After her death, Mueller preached a "funeral sermon" from Psalm 119:68, which says, "You are good, and do good." The three points of his message declared:

1. The Lord was good, and did good, in giving her to me.
2. The Lord was good, and did good, in so long leaving her to me.
3. The Lord was good and did good, in taking her from me.[13]

I still remember the darkest season of my ministry as if it were yesterday. I was a young pastor trying to lead a church that had gone through a disastrous staff moral failure, was experiencing massive financial problems, and was debilitated by all that had transpired. Their trust level was about as high as a shallow pond in the Mojave Desert. I learned quickly that hurting people hurt others and that the environment was cynical and unforgiving. My leadership stumbles in those early years did not help.

Mired in deep pain and disappointment, my wife and I dreamed about leaving ministry and finding a different career like a panhandler dreams of a night in the honeymoon suite of the Ritz Carlton. Yet I knew I still had choices. I could either fixate on what I saw in the circumstances and be defeated by what I felt emotionally, or anchor my well-being in what I knew to be true. I probably rehearsed it a thousand times over, "This looks bad. This feels bad. But God is good!" That truth saved my sanity and kept me in ministry to this day. Nahum 1:7 assures us, "The Lord is good, a stronghold in the day of trouble; he knows those who take refuge in him."

Mercy + Goodness = Forgiveness

God's mercy and goodness have brought us a great forgiveness. One of the excellent fruits of goodness is that we are compelled to forgive others. Unforgiveness reflects a failure to honor mercy because we want a self-justifying outcome. Unforgiveness ignores God's goodness because we feel we must control the relationship with negative emotion rather than believe in a good result. It's often been said that forgiveness does not make the other person right; it just makes us free—free to live in mercy and goodness. Unforgiveness is the poison we drink, expecting the other person to die. Forgiveness drinks from the fountain of life-giving mercy and triumphant goodness.

Mercy + Goodness = Security

As recipients of Christ's mercy and lovers of his goodness, we no longer have to engage in the insecure games of trying to look good or feel we are better than others. Rather than the "I can top that" game (my day was harder than your day, my life is more pitiful than your life, my kids are smarter than your kids), we can let the sure goodness of God fill our lives with security, selflessness, and servitude toward others.

Mercy + Goodness = Honor

We can actually begin to see others as recipients of God's mercy and goodness and treat them accordingly. Nothing is more void of mercy than when I have a cynical condemning spirit toward others. It is common to judge ourselves by our intentions and others by their actions, never giving them the benefit of the doubt and often suspecting the worst. But a life full of mercy and goodness brings a gracious understanding, a spirit of encouragement, and a new freedom to honor others above ourselves, imperfect as they are.

Mercy + Goodness = Endurance

A prayerful expectation and mercy-delivered experience of God's goodness keeps us from losing heart. David wrote, "I believe that I shall look upon the goodness of the Lord in the land of the living! Wait for the Lord; be strong, and let your heart take courage; wait for the Lord!" (Psalm 27:13–14). When Paul spoke of the blessings of the New Covenant of the gospel and the transformation we experience as we seek God, he was compelled to say, "Therefore, having this ministry by the mercy of God, we do not lose heart" (2 Corinthians 4:1). Yes, the fruit of mercy and the goodness of the gospel is evidenced in endurance.

Mercy + Goodness = Glory

The ultimate fruit of mercy and goodness is the glory of God in our lives. Jesus made it clear: "Let your light shine before others, so that they may see your good works and give glory to your Father who is in heaven" (Matthew 5:16). Romans 9:23–24 explains that God has worked "in order to make known the riches of his glory for vessels of mercy, which he has prepared beforehand for glory—even us whom he has called, not from the Jews only but also from the Gentiles." Merciless people, who see no good, hear no good, speak no good, and do no good are a miserable embarrassment to the glory of their creator.

Christ = Mercy + Goodness

The prophet Jeremiah speaks of a future "new covenant" that God would make with his people (Jeremiah 31:31). This included the new covenant that Jesus accomplished by his blood on the cross

(1 Corinthians 11:25; Hebrews 8:6–13). As John Piper states, "The benefits of this covenant reach as far as the blood of Jesus reaches."[14] As Christ-followers we are "fellow heirs [with Israel], members of the same body, and partakers of the promise in Christ Jesus through the gospel" (Ephesians 3:6). Jeremiah foretold that God would put his law in our hearts and that we would know him intimately because he would demonstrate his mercy by forgiving sin (Jeremiah 31:33–34).

In the next chapter, Jeremiah applied this covenant in further in detail:

> I will give them one heart and one way, that they may fear me forever, for their own *good* and the *good* of their children after them. I will make with them an everlasting covenant that I will not turn away from doing *good* to them. And I will put the fear of me in their hearts, that they may not turn from me. I will rejoice in doing them *good*, and I will plant them in this land in faithfulness, with all my heart and all my soul.
>
> Jeremiah 32:39–41

These promises, like a limitless buffet to a hungry soul, offer great assurance of the abundant goodness we have now experienced in Christ.

God changes our hearts and shows us his ways for our good and the good of our children. He has, does, and will do this in Christ. Also, God will not stop his goodness to us. As John Piper notes, "He keeps on doing good and he never will stop doing good for ten thousand ages of ages."[15]

Jeremiah tells us that God has great joy in doing good to us, even as a parent finds joy in the wedding day of a grown son who has found a virtuous wife. We read that God does good to us with all his heart and soul. This echoes what James promised, that God "gives generously to all and without reproach" (James 1:5). God will not waver or change his mind in his pledge of his goodness to us in Christ and the life of Christ's goodness in us (James 1:17).

Pray, Expect, and Produce Fruit

So call on God, my friend. He loves to answer your cry for this good wisdom and give you a life full of good fruits. In fact, the fruit of his Spirit is goodness (Galatians 5:22), so he loves to produce his character of goodness in and through you. This happens as we abide in Christ and he abides in us. Just as a branch draws life from the vine, so we draw from his goodness to produce much fruit (John 15:4–5).

As we continue in this life of abiding, through believing prayer, we will fulfill God's predetermined purpose to "be conformed to the image of his Son" (Romans 8:29). Our deepest needs will be met. Our life and relationships will never be the same.

A Story of His Goodness

A dear pastor friend of mine, Sandy Robertson, shared his heart with me recently. Even though he and his wife, Beth, lost a daughter in the prime of her life to cancer, they embraced God's goodness. Today, Beth and their daughter Brienne are enduring their own battles with cancer—surgery, chemo, and radiation. Still, they hold firmly to the goodness of God, trusting his love. He told me, "It's not always easy—but it is all we have and everything we need. Where else would we go and what else would we do if we did not anchor our soul in God's goodness?"

Not long ago, I visited with Sandy and some pastors from his area. As he and I drove together afterward, he recounted the following story that beautifully illustrates our need to trust the goodness and love of our God:

> I live on the Space Coast of Central Florida, about forty miles east of Orlando. One day my wife and I decided to surprise our eight-year-old granddaughter, Alexa, with a trip to Disney World. It was a national holiday and the schools were closed, so we picked her up early in the morning and off we went. She had no idea what we had planned. She thought it was going to be a day just hanging out with Grandma and Grandpa.
>
> Our first stop was McDonald's. We grabbed three Egg McMuffins at the drive-thru and then continued on our journey. Well, it just so happened that this McDonald's had a Playland attached to it. When Alexa saw that, she got excited and asked, "Grandpa, can we eat inside? I want to play."

"No, sweetheart," I replied. "We don't have time for that."

She then turned up the heat. "Please, Grandpa; I really want to go inside. I hardly ever get to come here. C'mon, Grandpa, why can't we eat inside? We've got time."

"Sorry, Alexa, the answer is no. We are doing the drive-thru."

Alexa was not a happy camper, and as expected, she fussed. She complained and then accused me of not letting her have any fun. That was followed by pouting and the silent treatment for the next half hour. We continued on our journey westward and at the appropriate moment, my wife declared, "Pull off somewhere, I need to find a restroom."

To this I replied, "Look, there's the sign for Disney World! I'll pull off here. They'll have public restrooms at Disney World."

As you can imagine, the wheels began to turn in Alexa's little brain. Then out came this sheepish voice from the backseat, "Grandpa, now that we are here at Disney World, do you think maybe we could go inside?"

"Of course we're going inside, Alexa. Grandma and I had this planned right from the beginning. But if you had had your way, you would have settled for McDonald's Playland."

What a memorable day we had together. We returned home that night exhausted and satisfied.

God is good. He is secretly planning in love and goodness for all of us. Don't be an Alexa. Don't settle for McDonald's Playland when God has Disney World in mind!

When we live according to the gospel wisdom of "good fruits," not only do we delight in God's ultimate "playland," but we become ambassadors to those who are settling for so much less, groveling in the cheap seats—and we are compelled to invite them to know the satisfying goodness of God in Christ.

Ready to Receive

What circumstance or relationship looks or feels bad in your life right now? Why does it seem that way? Do you truly believe that God's goodness is greater than the dynamics of this situation? Fix your mind on the character of God when you pray about this challenge, and ask Christ to show his overcoming goodness to you and through you. Be sure to thank him when things change.

Review John Piper's four goodness robbers listed on page 151. Which one of these would be your most commonly experienced thief? What specific truth in this chapter will equip you to be more receptive to Christ's prevailing goodness as you confront this robber in the coming days?

Reflect on the closing story told by Pastor Sandy Robertson. When have you fixated on a "McDonald's" experience only to find that God had a "Disney World" possibility in store for your life? What lessons can you apply to the specific situations of your life right now? Fix your eyes on Jesus today, trusting that he is good and will work that which is good in you, for you, and through you.

Take time to experience the following Wisdom Prayer, allowing the biblical truths to renew your mind as your prayerful response draws your heart closer to Christ, who is your wisdom.

Wisdom Prayer

The Goodness of Jesus

In Matthew 4:18–22. we see Jesus calling his first disciples (brothers Peter and Andrew along with brothers James and John). In verse 19, we see the essence of his call. After they immediately followed him, verses 23–25 give a picture of what they would be called to do as they are introduced to the nature of Jesus' goodness to all. This will provide guidance for our prayers along with the profound truths of Ephesians 2:10.

Matthew 4:19, 23–25

[19] And he said to them, "Follow me, and I will make you fishers of
men. . . ." [23] And he went throughout all Galilee, teaching in their
synagogues and proclaiming the gospel of the kingdom and healing
every disease and every affliction among the people. [24] So his fame
spread throughout all Syria, and they brought him all the sick, those
afflicted with various diseases and pains, those oppressed by demons,
epileptics, and paralytics, and he healed them. [25] And great crowds
followed him from Galilee and the Decapolis, and from Jerusalem
and Judea, and from beyond the Jordan.

Ephesians 2:10

[10] For we are his workmanship, created in Christ Jesus for good works, which God prepared beforehand, that we should walk in them.

REVERENCE—"Who is God?"

Lord Jesus, I praise you because . . .

- You have called me to follow you and given me an eternally significant purpose (Matthew 4:19)
- You have proclaimed the gospel of the kingdom to us (v. 23)
- In your goodness you address the deepest needs of mankind (v. 23)
- You bring healing to broken and rejected lives (v. 24)
- Your gospel has called people from every background, social status, and nation (v. 25)
- I am your workmanship (masterpiece/poem) (Ephesians 2:10)
- You have created new life in me (v. 10)
- You destined me to a life of good works (v. 10)

I praise you, Lord Jesus, that, because you have called me, you are making me ______________________ ["a fisher of men" PLUS other descriptions of your calling and identity]. (v. 19)

I praise you that because you have proclaimed the gospel of the kingdom (v. 23) to my heart, I ______________________ [benefits of your salvation].

RESPONSE—"How should I respond?"

I confess that I have not walked in the good works you have prepared for me, especially when I have encountered ______________________ ______________________ [descriptions of people in need]. (Matthew 4:24–25)

REQUESTS—"What should I pray about?"

Lord Jesus, help me manifest the wisdom of your good fruits, even as you did in your ministry, particularly when ______________________ [think of ministry opportunities to needy people].

Give me grace to see myself as you see me—a "masterpiece" (2:10)—so that . . .

- my spouse will see ______________________ [description of good works].
- my family will see ______________________ [description of good works].
- my neighbors will see ______________________ [description of good works].
- my co-workers will see ______________________ [description of good works].

READINESS—"Where am I headed?"

Give me your strength because ______________________________ [descriptions of spiritual attacks, distractions, etc.] often seem to derail my testimony of goodness in this world.

REVERENCE—"Who is God?"

I praise you that I have purpose in life because you have created new life in me. I know that when others see ______________________________ [descriptions of good works], they will glorify you. (Matthew 5:16)

10

How Wisdom Trumps Pride and Prejudice

But the wisdom from above is . . . impartial.

James 3:17

> Life comes with profound givens. God exists. God is impartial. God is and knows the truth. God has imprinted it on human hearts. It is knowable. We will be judged by it. Therefore life is not trivial. And our convictions about God and morality gain gravity and solidity and stability.[1]
>
> John Piper

My father-in-law was one of the most memorable individuals I ever knew. From the start he intimidated me as I was courting his youngest, and amazingly beautiful, daughter. In the eyes of a young seminarian, he was larger than life. A pastor for decades, denominational leader, and extraordinarily gifted preacher, Fred was hard to miss. His was a personality on steroids. Yes, he entered most rooms mouth first, but he left people blessed, enlivened, and encouraged.

One of his quirks was that he called each of his three daughters his "favorite"—but not in the presence of the other two. Of course when the daughters would get together they would each announce to the others that they were indeed his favorite.

Fred did it for fun. Some people actually have favorites in ways that are obvious to all and not very fun. Natural as this may be in a family, sports team, church staff, work group, or neighborhood—this is not wisdom from above.

Naturally, we all love to be favored by others. It might be as the teacher's pet, the player of the year, occupying the office next to the boss, hanging out with the pastor—or being called the favorite daughter. Special favor lets us feel good about ourselves, usually at the expense of everyone else, "inferior" as they may be.

But admit it: We're most often in the back of the line, far from the favored position. Like goldfish trying to survive in nuclear-waste water, we all feel the effect of a skewed and spiritually toxic environment of pride and prejudice that fuel partiality and strain relationships.

The Destructive Twins

Perhaps you've heard the account of June and Jennifer Gibbons detailed in the book *The Silent Twins* by Marjorie Wallace.[2] These identical twin girls, born in 1963 in Barbados, moved to Wales when they were young. Growing up, they were distinctly inseparable and soon developed their own way of communicating with each other.

At school they refused to read or write, and increasingly, their language became unintelligible to others. They sank into a strange and private world of simultaneous actions, which often mirrored each other. The twins' condition baffled psychiatrists, who described them as elective mutes.

In an attempt to break their interdependence, June and Jennifer were sent to separate boarding schools, but the pair became catatonic and entirely withdrawn when apart. After they were reunited, the two committed a number of crimes and were admitted to a high-security mental health center in England. Over the next fourteen years, they received regular high doses of antipsychotic medications. Although years earlier they had both written skillfully, they eventually were completely unable to concentrate. Their previous writings revealed unique dynamics of a love-hate relationship between the two.

After being transferred to a different hospital in 1993, Jennifer suddenly died. June went back to live with her parents in search for a normal, non-medicated life. The title of a *New York Times* article described them as "Bound Together in Fantasy and Crime."[3]

June and Jennifer Gibbons' story reminds us of how the twin maladies of pride and prejudice affect us in many destructive ways. Often this is replicated in our lifestyles and relationships. Pride and prejudice are indeed bound together, leading us to a fantasy of self-centered living and ungodly behaviors, evidenced in our relationships.

God's Impartial and Harmonious Provision

The greater reality that trumps pride and prejudice is the assurance that God loves to make you impartial because he is impartial, as we will see in a moment. James encourages us to pray for the wisdom from above that is impartial.

A common dictionary definition of *impartial* would suggest that it is the idea of being fair or just. *Partiality* is bias that prefers one over another. *Favoritism* is showing advantageous treatment of some while neglecting others.

The New Testament word can also mean "unwavering," "harmonious," "not doubting," "not given to a party spirit," and "without uncertainty or inconsistency." Conversely, one Greek word used to describe "partiality" literally means "face receiving"—or judging by externals.[4] One commentator notes, "These meanings are relatively close to one another: the person with true wisdom is apparently nonpartisan: instead he is pure and absolutely sincere in his opinions and actions."[5]

Partiality is a self-centered view of relationships. Impartiality is a God-centered view of relationships. We are usually partial based on superficial markers, not spiritual measurements. We are partial based on how we want people to view us, rather than resting in how God views us. We are partial as a reaction to how others treat us rather than as a resolve about how God wants us to treat them. At the core of favoritism and partiality we find the symbiotic connection between pride and prejudice.

But when we value people as God does, we can be unwavering in our relationships. When we are secure in our own worth before God, we can base our treatment of others on spiritual measurements and steer clear of favoritism. When we treat people according the wisdom from above, we can live a harmonious existence.

Our Impartial God

There is no sinful partiality in God. In Job 34:19, we read that God "shows no partiality to princes, nor regards the rich more than the poor, for they are all the work of his hands." God is not impressed with wealth or unimpressed with poverty. Second Chronicles 19:7 says, "Let the fear of the Lord be upon you. Be careful what you do, for there is no injustice with the Lord our God, or partiality or taking bribes." God cannot be in any way persuaded by money or power. Ephesians 6:8–9 warns those who are in authority to be fair to all, "knowing that whatever good anyone does, this he will receive back from the Lord, whether he is a bondservant or is free. Masters, do the same to them, and stop your threatening, knowing that he who is both their Master and yours is in heaven, and that there is no partiality with him." God does not favor status, position, or human titles. He does not give special allowance to the misbehavior of the boss. He does not see as man sees. Rather, he looks on the heart and always evaluates, judges, and rewards fairly. First Samuel 16:7 reminds us, "For the Lord sees not as man sees: man looks on the outward appearance, but the Lord looks on the heart."

In his display of common grace on mankind, God is impartial: "For he makes his sun rise on the evil and on the good, and sends rain on the just and on the unjust" (Matthew 5:45). On the other hand, God is also unprejudiced in his divine judgment of each person. Based on his holy character, absolute truth, and perfect knowledge of every individual's response to his universally revealed moral law, he will judge fairly. In this light, Romans 2:11 says, "For God shows no partiality."

This is important. Many Christians I have met live as if God will judge them on a curve because they think they are more exceptional than others. Yes, we are loved, but we are also all accountable to an eternally established moral standard. As believers, we know that Christ has satisfied that standard for us at the cross in respect to our eternal salvation. But we also know that we will be accountable for what we have done in this life and will be evaluated with no favoritism in eternity at the judgment seat of Christ. Second Corinthians 5:9–10 says, "So whether we are at home or away, we make it our aim to please him. For we must all appear before the judgment seat of Christ, so that each one may receive what is due for what he has done in the body, whether good or evil."

God Choose Some?

But you may have already wondered—why did God choose Jacob over Esau, David over Saul, or Israel over other nations? Why did Jesus spend more time with Peter, James, and John, with John being labeled as "the disciple that Jesus loved"? Aren't these evidences of favoritism? Romans chapter 9 addresses our fallen viewpoints and accusations against God's plans. His designs may seem unfair to our limited understanding. The answer is that God is sovereign and chooses people, places, and events based on his perfect knowledge and eternal plan that was established before the creation of man. We are the clay. He is the potter. Ultimately he does all things "in order to make known the riches of his glory for vessels of mercy, which he has prepared beforehand for glory"(Romans 9:23).

So here is a tension. The Bible makes it clear that he is impartial in how he views people. He is impartial in how he applies his standard of truth to every life. He is impartial in rewarding us. He alone is God, sovereign, all-knowing, and eternal. News flash: We are not! We do not know the big picture of his purposes, nor are we always motivated by his glory. We are fallen but redeemed vessels of mercy.

Our need is to embrace his revealed wisdom and seek his honor in all our relationships. The rest we leave in his perfect hands. We know he calls us to be impartial, and that is our ultimate responsibility, our joy, and our accountability in this life.

Dissecting and Overcoming Partiality

In the book of James, the writer identifies two specific violations of this wisdom-trait. The first one he addresses in detail in chapter 2. Like the cliquish conversational circles at an elite dinner party, believers in the churches to which James wrote were exhibiting favoritism in their gatherings.

> My brothers, show no partiality as you hold the faith in our Lord Jesus Christ, the Lord of glory. For if a man wearing a gold ring and fine clothing comes into your assembly, and a poor man in shabby clothing also comes in, and if you pay attention to the one who wears the fine clothing and say, "You sit here in a good place," while you say to the poor man, "You stand over there," or, "Sit down at my feet," have you not then made distinctions among yourselves and become judges with evil thoughts?
>
> James 2:1–4

James candidly illustrates what can become so common and culturally acceptable in our society and even our Christian interactions. As he writes, he confirms that partiality and favoritism are motivated by sinful aspirations. The recipients of James' message were overtly honoring and elevating the rich while diminishing the poor. Forgetting that the ground is level at the foot of the cross, they were erecting man-made pedestals of different sizes to elevate the ones that the world deemed successful. This was a blatant contradiction of the grace of the cross.

Proverbs 22:2 tells us, "Rich and poor have this in common: The Lord is the Maker of them all" (NIV). He is also the savior of both, and his blood shed for the outcast was of no less value than his sacrifice for a king. Paul commands us, "Live in harmony with one another. Do not be haughty, but associate with the lowly. Never be wise in your own sight" (Romans 12:16). There is no place for pride and prejudice in the kingdom of Jesus, subtle and socially acceptable as it might seem.

Privileged Participants?

And while we are on this, let's be honest—many of these "privileged" people expect special treatment. I remember working for a ministry where I was interfacing with a very wealthy supporter as part of my job. He had given millions to this ministry but had developed a rather aberrant view of some points of theology. He eventually told the leadership of the organization that if they did not adopt his viewpoints, he would pull his money. With shekels come shackles.

Yet this kind of thing is rampant in the church and nonprofit Christian enterprises. Fundraisers tell us that we must give special treatment to the big donors. While we want our hearts to be pure in expressing gratitude, crossing that line of overt favoritism is subtle and easy to do.

This reminds me of the story of Simon the Sorcerer in Acts 8. He believed the message of the gospel but apparently still wanted some preferential treatment in acquiring special powers from the disciples. The story tells us, "He offered them money, saying, 'Give me this power also, so that anyone on whom I lay my hands may receive the Holy Spirit'" (Acts 8:18–19). But Peter said to him, "May your silver perish with you, because you thought you could obtain the gift of God with money! You have neither part nor lot in this matter, for your heart is not right before God" (8:20–21). Eugene Peterson translates it in *The Message*, "To hell with your money! And you along with it. Why, that's unthinkable—trying to buy God's gift!" Strong words but essential if we are serious about this wisdom from above.

Later in his teaching James speaks candidly about some of these honored wealthy participants when he says, "Are not the rich the ones who oppress you, and the ones who drag you into court? Are they not the ones who blaspheme the honorable name by which you were called?" (James 2:6–7). Admittedly, he is speaking about the behaviors of the wealthy that do not honor God in their lives. Apparently they still attended church in these settings. James reveals that they used their influence to oppress and even reject God. That is the sad effect of the "love of money" (see 1 Timothy 6:10) apart from the saving grace of the gospel.

Rich, Poor, and Honoring Both

Let me say that if you are wealthy and reading this, pray for a godly spirit of impartiality. Do not fall into the trap of allocating your riches based on what people do for you, how they recognize you, or how they pay you special attention. In Luke 6:32–34, Jesus pointed out that even the pagans treat people based on how they are treated. Christians have a higher standard and calling. Make your stewardship decisions based on a deep-rooted surrender to Christ and his gospel. Give for eternal reward and the pleasure of God because he is the source of all you have.

If you are poor, pray that people will see you through God's eyes, but also ask for the grace to see the wealthy through God's eyes, not despising them because of their riches. See your self-worth not based on net worth, but on your worth to God, who valued you so much that he gave his son for you. And do not covet, but be content with gratefulness to God's grace and for his purposes in your unique mission in this life.

If you are a ministry leader, be careful. Pray for this wisdom. God wants to give it to you and will be pleased with you—even if some do not understand. His support is far better than that of any human benefactor.

Beyond Evil to a Wise Evaluation

James makes it clear: "Have you not then made distinctions among yourselves and become judges with evil thoughts?" (James 2:4). The Bible tells us that it is sinful to make distinctions based on earthly measurements. We set ourselves up as judges, ignoring the plumb line of God's holy evaluation of men, and have trumped his wisdom with our cockeyed pride and prejudice. We cannot determine our treatment of people based on personal gain regardless of whether it is to bolster our self-worth, grow our organizations, or get in on a share of special luxuries.

Next James writes, "Listen, my beloved brothers, has not God chosen those who are poor in the world to be rich in faith and heirs of the kingdom, which he has promised to those who love him? But you have dishonored the poor man" (v. 5–6). He calls believers to see people from God's perspective—not based on some façade but on faith. We want to honor those "rich in faith." This is important because without faith it is impossible to please God (Hebrews 11:6).

Love = Impartiality

In the book of Galatians, believers were getting wrapped up on another issue of superficial concern. It was not about external appearances of wealth but external appearances of religious devotion. Paul cuts to the core issue when he writes, "For in Christ Jesus neither circumcision nor uncircumcision counts for anything, but only faith working through love" (Galatians 5:6). James parallels this truth. In Christ Jesus, neither wealth nor poverty counts for anything but *faith working through love.* That is the place of real favor and honor.

See how James now underscored this:

> If you really fulfill the royal law according to the Scripture, "You shall love your neighbor as yourself," you are doing well. But if you show partiality, you are committing sin and are convicted by the law as transgressors. For whoever keeps the whole law but fails in one point has become accountable for all of it.
>
> James 2:8–10

Our motivation in relating to others is love. We love others, even as we love ourselves, and more important, even as we are loved by Christ (John 13:34; Ephesians 5:2). It should not matter if they are rich or poor, talented or under-skilled, pleasant or melancholy, bright or daft, beautiful or unsightly, educated or a drop-out. They may compliment us or ignore us. They may encourage us or exasperate us. The truth is that we are not the point of reference. Christ's love for them is the standard.

And how serious is this matter? James says that by showing partiality, these folks were committing sin and convicted as transgressors (2:9). John MacArthur describes the distinction of these two terms: "*Harmartia*, translated simply *sin*, pertains to missing the mark of God's standard of righteousness, whereas *parabates [transgressors]* refers to someone who willingly goes beyond God's prescribed limits. In the one case, a person comes short; in the other, he goes too far."[6] Perhaps their prejudice in dishonoring some was coming up short. Perhaps the pride of superficially elevating others was going too far.

James went on to specify that two of the most heinous relational sins, adultery and murder, are no more serious than the sin of partiality (2:11). God's mercy is over it all in Christ, but his passage is a foghorn blast to our complacent hearts. Oh, how we need the wisdom from above that is impartial.

Influence and Impartiality

It is also good to remember a second evidence of partiality that had crept into the churches of the day as James writes. This kind was based on position and knowledge. In James 3:1, he calls out the influential teachers who expect special esteem based on their teaching roles. James turns the tables by telling them they will actually face a stronger evaluation by God because of their supposed knowledge. Much of what leads into this great section about the wisdom from above in James 3 was the misuse of their position to justify destructive words and as a cover for sinful relational behavior. That's why James condemns sins of the tongue (3:1–2) and sets the standard for real honor as "the deeds done in the humility that comes from wisdom" (3:13 NIV).

In churches today, people still express and expect favoritism based on position, desired prominence, and even history in the church. They seek to manipulate in order to have special privilege and power. I call them "stockholders" because they think that because of their years of service, tenure of membership, doctrinal superiority, or even regular giving that they deserve more attention, position, and a louder voice than a new convert. Another news flash: There is no stock available in the church. Jesus bought the church with his own blood and owns it all (Acts 20:28). Both their expectations and any deference to it can only be classified as sin. In leadership and ministry, we cannot show favoritism. Paul underscored the seriousness of this when he told Timothy, "In the presence of God and of Christ Jesus and of the elect angels I charge you to keep these rules without prejudging, doing nothing from partiality" (1 Timothy 5:21).

Impartial Jesus

As this verse just stated, our impartiality is motivated by the presence of Jesus. Like a bucket with a hole in it, this chapter would not have integrity unless we honored the model of our impartial Savior.

This Lord of Glory selected common fishermen and a despised tax collector for his inner circle. This was a clue to the impartial nature of his entire ministry. Author Michael Griffiths explains,

> Jesus will dine with the despised and the honored, with friends and with adversaries and critics. He speaks out for the poor, but he does not ostracize the rich. . . . He did not disregard strangers and foreigners from outside Israel. He was ready to relate to the Roman centurion and the Syrophoenician woman. He was ready to talk to the sinful Samaritan woman, the demented man from whom others fled, and to touch the defiled leper. . . . All sorts of people seemed to be drawn to Jesus as by a magnet. He never seemed to have been too busy for people or to be rushed or flustered.[7]

Observing the heart and life of Jesus compels us to a true undivided loyalty to him for the good of all those who are *objects* of his love.

Thus Jesus lives in us and imparts to us a truly impartial heart. Seeing people through eyes other than the unbiased and loving eyes of Jesus is a total violation of the heart and model of the object of our worship gatherings—Jesus himself. This was the challenge offered by James, and one needful for us.

Heart, Home, and the House of God

So how do we apply all of this? No surprise, it comes back to Jesus, the life spring of impartial wisdom. Take a moment to read these familiar verses, perhaps in a new light.

> So if there is any encouragement in Christ, any comfort from love, any participation in the Spirit, any affection and sympathy, complete my joy by being of the same mind, having the same love, being in full accord and of one mind. Do nothing from selfish ambition or conceit, but in humility count others more significant than yourselves. Let each of you look not only to his own interests, but also to the interests of others. Have this mind among yourselves, which is yours in Christ Jesus.
>
> Philippians 2:1–5

Our motive and goal is to have the mind of Christ and demonstrate self-sacrificing love in all relationships. So in closing, here are a few applications:

1. In every relationship, we must trust God to help us see people through his eyes—as souls who are the object of his love, regardless of the outer packaging.
2. In our marriages, we must avoid all superficial comparisons that might classify our spouse in some inferior way based on the looks, abilities, status, achievement, or personality of some other person.
3. In our homes, we must pray for the wisdom to treat each of our children with consistent godly love, respect, encouragement, and value. We must avoid parental interaction or sibling rivalries that attribute value based on talent, intelligence, personality, or achievement.
4. In ministry, we must honor our impartial Christ, remembering his approach to people during his earthy ministry, and avoid using others based on what they can do for us or our efforts.
5. In society, we must endeavor to seek justice and mercy for all people, as eternally significant souls, especially the downtrodden and outcast.

6. In evangelism, we can appeal to the impartiality of both God's judgment of sin and offer of salvation, remembering that even those far from Christ are not the enemy but victims of the enemy.

Ready to Receive

Remembering that partiality involves judging people by externals, what external factors typically cause you to judge other people? Why do you think this occurs? What truths in this chapter have challenged your tendencies? What changes could the wisdom of Jesus produce in you in the future?

Do you ever tend to expect partial treatment from others based on your financial status, position in life, education, or for any other reason? What fuels this expectation? How would the mind of Christ change this expectation? Looking at your calendar for the coming weeks, pray specifically about how you can exhibit the mind of Christ in place of your previous expectations.

Review the six application points just presented. Which of these seems most timely for you as you apply the impartial wisdom of the gospel? Prayerfully plan to make this application in an upcoming conversation or gathering.

Take time to experience the following Wisdom Prayer, allowing the biblical truths to renew your mind as your prayerful response draws your heart closer to Christ, who is your wisdom.

Wisdom Prayer

Jesus, the Impartial

Jesus' entire life and ministry was a demonstration of impartiality as he served people selflessly and with no considerations for superficial labels, backgrounds, or positions in life. The story in Mark 12:38–44 is just one example of this and will help us as we pray.

Mark 12:38–44

38 And in his teaching he said, "Beware of the scribes, who like to walk around in long robes and like greetings in the marketplaces 39 and have the best seats in the synagogues and the places of honor at feasts, 40 who devour widows' houses and for a pretense make long prayers. They will receive the greater condemnation." 41 And he sat down opposite the treasury and watched the people putting money into the offering box. Many rich people put in large sums. 42 And a poor widow came and put in two small copper coins, which make a penny. 43 And he called his disciples to him and said to them, "Truly, I say to you, this poor widow has put in more than all those who are contributing to the offering box. 44 For they all contributed out of their abundance, but she out of her poverty has put in everything she had, all she had to live on."

REVERENCE—"Who is God?"

Lord Jesus, I praise you because . . .

- You see the heart, not the outward appearance of our lives (vv. 38–39)
- You will someday judge all injustice and superficiality (v. 40)
- You watch and know the nature of our service and giving to you (vv. 41–42)
- You are an advocate of the widow (vv. 42–43)
- You value not the amount of the gift but the sincerity of the sacrifice (v. 43)

I praise you, Lord Jesus, that you knew my heart and confronted my religious superficiality when I ______________________________. (v. 41)

I praise you, Lord Jesus, that it mattered to you when I gave you ______________ [description of your genuine sacrifice for him]. (vv. 43–44)

RESPONSE—"How should I respond?"

I confess that, like the scribes, (vv. 38–40) I have expected special treatments and man's honor when ______________ ______________. I confess this as sin and seek a new empowerment of your impartial wisdom.

I confess that I have often been partial to people who appear to be more important and have disregarded those who appear to be the least. Rather than a focus on outward things, give me your eyes to see ______________.

REQUESTS—"What should I pray about?"

Lord, knowing you see my heart, deliver me from the spiritual pretense of the scribes when I am tempted to ______________.

Give me eyes to see people as you see them, that I will more sincerely honor ______________ [categories of people—like widows—or specific people who come to mind].

READINESS—"Where am I headed?"

As I live in a world of superficial measurements, deliver me from trying to "make an impression" when ______________, and rather to humbly sacrifice ______________ for you.

REVERENCE—"Who is God?"

I praise you that you honor and delight in the sacrifice of the heart, and I declare that you are worthy of my ______________.

11

Wise Guys (and Gals) Are the Real Deal

But the wisdom from above is . . . sincere.

James 3:17

There is a wholeness to true wisdom that brings heart and head, feeling and thoughts, deeds and words together.[1]

David Hubbard

There is a sad, sarcastic adage that says, "The key to leadership is sincerity. Once you learn to fake that, you've got it made." No one would overtly announce this as a core value of life. Yet in reality, too many are drawn to that kind of persona. Social media fuels a sense of superficiality in life and relationships. We post largely what we want others to see or read about us in order to think of us in a positive, even envious light. Our online identity and our true identity can be grossly misaligned. In today's media-driven world, the seeds of hypocrisy commonly fall on fertile soil. This is why we must pray daily for wisdom from above that is sincere.

Tragic Heroes

The Greek philosopher Aristotle spoke of the role of the "tragic hero" in the classic dramas of his day. This was a person who rose to notable heights only to experience a spectacular fall. In each case, the character exhibited a fatal flaw that led to his or her ruin. Sadly, this literary imagery is real-life stuff in today's society, and in proportions that baffle the mind and barrage our relationships. At the core of every newsworthy or unreported common-life reputational and relational meltdown, you will always find the spoiling ingredient of hypocrisy. Like undetected black mold in a home, hypocrisy can grow quietly, producing a contaminated life environment and ailing relationships.

Twice in my pastoral ministry I was called to serve as the senior pastor of a large congregation that had just experienced the heartbreak of a long-term pastor caught in adultery. These are not the kind of assignments you dream about in seminary. Like the rescue crew following a 7.5 earthquake in a large city, I spent a lot of time sorting through relational rubble, trying to rescue disenfranchised souls and trusting God for the strength to rebuild something that would honor Christ and withstand future hardships. I learned firsthand about the fallout that occurs in lives and homes in the wake of a "tragic hero" story.

Big Life, Big Fail—Common Lives, Common Fails

One of the sport's world's most recognizable figures is Lance Armstrong, the cyclist who won the Tour de France seven consecutive times from 1999 to 2005.

The popular 2015 film *The Program* portrayed his world-renowned rise and fall after an Irish sports journalist eventually discovered evidence that exposed Armstrong's dark and deceitful hypocrisy. This became the most famous sports doping scandal in history. In 2012, the U.S. Anti-Doping Agency compiled a huge file of evidence against him and subsequently banned him from cycling for life while also revoking his Tour de France titles.

In January 2013, Armstrong finally publicly confessed to doping during a televised interview with Oprah Winfrey. In that conversation, Armstrong unequivocally admitted for the first time that his Tour de

France titles had been unjustly won. "It's just this mythic, perfect story, and it isn't true," he said.[2]

Armstrong was also a celebrated cancer survivor. Over time, he even used that story and his Livestrong Foundation efforts as a cover for his hypocrisy. David Walsh, the reporter whose efforts led to Armstrong's exposure, commented, "'Cancer survivor' was an adjective that, for good or ill, followed Armstrong wherever he went. The bit Lance will find hard to reconcile with himself will be the way he lied to the cancer community. . . . He set up his foundation and did a lot of good work, but he also used his cancer work as a shield—no question about that. He knew the lie he was telling. . . . When Lance lied, he lied very convincingly."[3]

Stephen Frears, director of *The Program*, commented about Armstrong, "I don't think he's a particularly self-reflective person. You have to be a certain kind of person to lie on that scale." When Armstrong spoke to CNN in 2014 about his doping denials, he admitted he "was good at playing the part. Once you say 'no' you have to keep saying 'no.' If this stuff hadn't taken place with the federal investigation, I'd probably still be saying 'no' with the same conviction and tone as before."[4]

Armstrong's story warns us of the miserable fallout of hypocrisy. Most "genuine article" failures never make the news, but we know them well. We just have to look around at church, the office, or the neighborhood. Or even in the mirror.

Well-known pastor Charles Edward Jefferson wrote a century ago:

> And yet how common insincerity is. What a miserable old humbug of a world we are living in, full of trickery and dishonesty and deceit of every kind. Society is cursed with affectation, business is honeycombed with dishonesty, the political world abounds in duplicity and chicanery, there is sham and pretense everywhere. . . . The life of many a man and many a woman is one colossal lie. We say things we do not mean, express emotions we do not feel, praise when we secretly condemn, smile when there is a frown on the face of the heart, give compliments when we are thinking curses. We strive a hundred times a week to make people think we are other than we really are.[5]

Sincerely Wise

Against the dark human backdrop of our gargantuan duplicity, James delivers dazzling radiance from heaven with the truth that the wisdom from above makes us sincere. This word *sincere* literally means "not playing a part" and "being free from pretense or deceit."

The word originated from the world of Greek drama. It described the masks actors used to dramatize multiple characters in the same play. Still today a symbol of the theater is the twin masks of comedy and tragedy.

To be sincere is to live a life "without masks." One commentator has noted, "The person characterized by wisdom from heaven will be stable, trustworthy, transparent—the kind of person consistently displaying the virtues of wisdom and on whom one can rely for advice and counsel."[6] Another writer adds, "For such a person could not pretend or playact in order to influence people, but would act alike toward all. He would indeed be inspired by God and be a binding force in the Christian community."[7]

Charles Edward Jefferson speaks beautifully again:

> Thank God there are hearts here and there upon which we can depend. . . . It is to the honest heart that we return again and again, seeking rest and finding it. It is a fountain at which we drink and refresh ourselves for the toilsome journey. Beautiful, indeed, is the virtue of sincerity. It is not a gaudy virtue. It does not glitter. It has no sparkle in it. But it is substantial. It is life-giving. It sustains and nourishes the heart. . . . There are some things we cannot be, and many things we cannot do. But this one thing is within the reach of us all—we may ask God unceasingly to keep our heart sincere.[8]

Heart Problems

"Beautiful, indeed, is the virtue of sincerity," says Jefferson. How could we disagree? Who among us does not want to be that trusted heart to whom friends return again and again? True believers long to be and to find the fountains of sincerity in others from which they can drink and be refreshed. And yes, it is within reach as James reminds us, coming from God "who gives generously without reproach." So why does the attainment of it seem so attractive but so arduous?

Simply, we have a heart problem. Jeremiah 17:9 tells us, "The heart is deceitful above all things, and desperately sick; who can understand it?" Imagine going to a doctor about a chronic physical difficulty and being diagnosed as a lost cause and rotten to the core. This would be devastating. Here, Jeremiah not only exposes the rebellious hearts of the unbelieving Jewish people but the condition of every person living without Christ. Solomon concurred, "The hearts of the children of man are full of evil, and madness is in their hearts while they live" (Ecclesiastes 9:3).

Paul described the depravity of men's souls apart from Christ as being "dead in the trespasses and sins" and "darkened in their understanding, alienated from the life of God because of the ignorance that is in them, due to their hardness of heart" (Ephesians 2:1; 4:18). Hypocrisy flourishes in a darkened heart like a slimy worm feeding under a rock.

In the face of the Pharisees' arguments about the legality of certain eating habits based on their traditions, Jesus called them out by saying, "This people honors me with their lips, but their heart is far from me" (Mark 7:6). Then he explained that it is not what goes in the mouth to the stomach that defiles a person but what comes out of the mouth from the heart. "For from within, out of the heart of man, come evil thoughts, sexual immorality, theft, murder, adultery, coveting, wickedness, deceit, sensuality, envy, slander, pride, foolishness. All these evil things come from within, and they defile a person" (Mark 7:21–23). So we see that hypocrisy is a heart problem. That is why we so desperately need the saving grace of the One who is "the way, and the truth, and the life" (John 14:6).

But here is a more riveting reality for church folks like me. We can still deceive ourselves even with the knowledge of Christ. Here are some examples:

- When we think that embracing the world's wisdom improves us, we deceive ourselves. (1 Corinthians 3:18)
- When we proudly overestimate our self-importance, we deceive ourselves. (Galatians 6:3)

- When we think that our actions do not have consequences (for better or for worse), we deceive ourselves. (Galatians 6:7)
- When we deny the sinful nature of our disobedience, we deceive ourselves. (1 John 1:8)

And James has already tagged us earlier in his letter:

- If we think we are okay in just hearing the truth but not obeying it, we deceive ourselves. (James 1:22)
- If we are religious but allow destructive speech, we deceive ourselves. (James 1:26)

All of this is not to discourage but to compel us to recognize our great need of a sincere heart and our great Christ who can make it so. Proverbs 28:26 affirms, "Whoever trusts in his own mind is a fool, but he who walks in wisdom will be delivered." All glory to Christ by whose life we can walk in wisdom and be delivered from hypocrisy and self-deception!

In 1 Timothy, Paul instructed his son in the faith, "The aim of our charge is love that issues from a pure heart and a good conscience and a sincere faith" (1:5). God has given us a compelling goal to live a life of love for him and others, with a conscious alert to all deception, so that we will have a sincere faith, void of hypocrisy.

How Now?

So how do we now live in the power of divine wisdom that transcends hypocrisy and empowers sincerity?

A Sincere Savior

Again, I love the words of Jefferson:

> Would you see sincerity in its loveliest form, then come to Jesus. Here is a man incapable of a lie. Nothing was as abhorrent to him as falsehood. No other people so stirred his wrath as men who pretended to be what they were not. The most odious word upon his lips was

> "hypocrite." Have you ever wondered why it is impossible to speak that word without it falling from the lips like a serpent—it is because his curse is resting on it. . . . He breathed the hot breath of his scorn into it, and it has been ever since a word degraded and lost.[9]

Jesus is the truth that sets us free. His life in us convicts of hypocrisy and delivers soul-deep sincerity. As one writer has noted, "God hates hypocrisy but loves sinners. In all the records of the Gospels, Jesus spoke to sinners with sympathy, kindness, and forgiveness. But to the hypocritical religious leaders, He used the strongest possible language of condemnation."[10] We dare not harbor hypocrisy but unreservedly confess our sins, knowing that he is faithful and just to forgive when we agree with him rather than hide from his all-knowing truth. This is the path to knowing, experiencing, and honoring our sincere Savior.

The Power of Truth

Like an unforgettable movie is the Old Testament story of King David, who coddled hypocrisy in a series of bizarre violations of relationships, followed by a masquerade of colossal magnitude. After an affair with beautiful Bathsheba, then the setup of the murder of her husband, a trusted soldier in his army, David went to bed every night not just with a new woman, but with the haunting harlot of his own hypocrisy. Scholars believe that David lived with this duplicity for well over a year before he was confronted by the prophet Nathan (see 2 Samuel 12:1–15). The core of Nathan's confrontation was that David had "despised the word of the Lord" (v. 9).

You may know that the consequences of David's sin and hypocrisy were extraordinary. In keeping with his promise, the Lord allowed David and Bathsheba's sin-conceived son to die. As Nathan also promised, David had trouble from his own household. In time, David's son Amnon raped David's daughter, Tamar. David's other son, Absalom, avenged the rape of his sister by killing Amnon (2 Samuel 13:28–29). Absalom, embittered by the now broken relationship with his dad, eventually led a coup against David, taking control of the kingdom and even openly having sex with David's wives. Like a seedy soap opera, things unraveled at several points, reminding us of the consequences of harbored hypocrisy.

But here is the point—and the great news for us: David responded to the truth when confronted. He was spared and forgiven. All of Psalm 51 bares his prayer of confession. At the core of it we find this admission, "Behold, you delight in truth in the inward being, and you teach me wisdom in the secret heart" (Psalm 51:6). There we see it, truth received and wisdom applied at the core of our being. Hypocrisy is banished. Sincerity surges forward. Freedom.

Later, while exiled by the rebellion of Absalom, David reaffirmed the priority of a truth-receptive heart when he wrote, "O Lord, who shall sojourn in your tent? Who shall dwell on your holy hill? He who walks blamelessly and does what is right and speaks truth in his heart" (Psalm 15:1–2). Intimacy with God is reflected in a blameless life, crafted by doing the right thing, springing from the core of a truth-embracing heart.

God provides wisdom from above in direct relation to our receptivity and obedience to his word. His living Word works powerfully within us, like a razor-sharp sword penetrating the thoughts and motives of our hearts. Authenticity is our compelling response when we know that "no creature is hidden from his sight, but all are naked and exposed to the eyes of him to whom we must give account" (Hebrews 4:13). Paul's ministry was marked by this word-embracing sincerity, "For we are not, like so many, peddlers of God's word, but as men of sincerity, as commissioned by God, in the sight of God we speak in Christ" (2 Corinthians 2:17).

Peter encourages all of us to embrace the connection between sincerity and the power of God's word in our lives by putting away "all deceit and hypocrisy." Then the connection—"like newborn infants, long for the pure spiritual milk, that by it you may grow up into salvation—if indeed you have tasted that the Lord is good" (1 Peter 2:1–3). As a result, we experience Christ building us up by his life in us, to become a spiritual and holy people for his pleasure (1 Peter 2:4–5).

Authentic Relationships

Few things undermine marriages, families, and friendships over time more than the donning of masks. When you cannot truly know and be known, superficiality and dissonance stick out like cheap, mismatched spray paint on a damaged car bumper. Quoting the apostle Peter again, we see him connecting truth, sincerity, and loving relationships: "Having purified your souls by your obedience to the truth for a sincere brotherly love, love one another earnestly from a pure heart" (1 Peter 1:22). Romans 12:9 calls us to something much richer and sweeter than faking it to try to make it: "Let love be genuine [without hypocrisy]. Abhor what is evil; hold fast to what is good."

Even in professional or more distanced relationships, sincerity is a powerful force. Paul clarified, "[Slaves], obey in everything those who are your earthly masters, not by way of eye-service, as people-pleasers, but with sincerity of heart, fearing the Lord" (Colossians 3:22). The Christ-honoring health of these relationships springs from sincerity, rooted in a fear of the Lord—a reverence and submission to Jesus.

A Fearless Life

Hypocrites live in fear. The fear of being found out. The potential trauma of being exposed. This fear is a snare and the opposite of the fear of the Lord. It's been said that it takes seven additional lies to cover up the first one. While not scientific, it is functionally true. A liar must have a very good memory to recall who he told, what he told, when he told, and why he told his half-truths. This again cultivates a personally and relationally destructive fear.

Like Adam and Eve in the Garden who hid themselves from the presence of the Lord, hypocrites hide behind masks. Job, in seeking to express the integrity of his heart, denied hypocrisy: "If I have concealed my transgressions as others do by hiding my iniquity in my heart, because I stood in great fear of the multitude, and the contempt of families terrified me, so that I kept silence, and did not go out of doors" (31:33–34). Notice his insight as he admits that sin would have made him hide. Fear would have kept him secluded.

The wisdom from above makes us courageous because it frees us from hypocrisy and hiding. Paul proclaimed the power of this reality in his life and ministry, "For our boast is this, the testimony of our conscience, that we behaved in the world with simplicity and godly sincerity, not by earthly wisdom but by the grace of God, and supremely so toward you" (2 Corinthians 1:12). Freed from fear and with confidence springing from his assured sincerity of his life and ministry, Paul affirmed his legacy among the Corinthians. This leads us to the final fruit of a wisely genuine life.

An Untarnished Legacy

After saving us, God has left us here on a mission to reproduce the wisdom from above in other disciples, which would include family, friends, and associates. I say often that an inheritance is what we leave for others; a legacy is what we leave in them.[11] I remember John Maxwell saying that success is when the people who know you best respect you the most. This is the impact of a mask-free life.

Paul urged his disciple and associate Titus to leave a legacy of sincerity. "In all things you yourself must be an example of good behavior. Be sincere and serious in your teaching" (Titus 2:7 GNT). He prayed for his disciples in Philippi similarly: "For I want you to understand what really matters, so that you may live pure and blameless lives until the day of Christ's return. May you always be filled with the fruit of your salvation—the righteous character produced in your life by Jesus Christ—for this will bring much glory and praise to God" (Philippians 1:10–11 NLT). A genuine life of righteous character produced by Christ! Wisdom from above. (We will look at the fruit of righteous character in the next and final chapter.)

We must at least notice the legacy of sincerity that was deposited in Timothy's life. Yes, we presume by Paul, but for certain by two wise women. Paul wrote to Timothy, "I am reminded of your sincere faith, a faith that dwelt first in your grandmother Lois and your mother Eunice and now, I am sure, dwells in you as well" (2 Timothy 1:5). Wisdom from above, seen in the fruit of sincere faith, transmitted through three generations. Lois and Eunice will forever be esteemed for their final performance: Timothy. A new generation of sincere faith. This was their legacy, and it can be yours—and mine.

Prayers of Truth and Transformation

So ask God for a sincere life. He wants to answer that prayer. In my book *Transforming Prayer*, I help readers understand that prayer is not just therapeutic. Prayer is transformational. We do not simply seek God's hand for temporary help, but we seek his face for a changed heart. Yes, he cares about our practical needs, but he wants to change us into the image of Christ as we pray. With our eyes on Jesus—the epitome of truth, sincerity, love, and courage—let us seek the life-change he loves to impart. We will be transformed into the real deal, from glory to glory, by the power of the Spirit of God in us.

Today, too many use the excuse that they are not interested in following Christ because of all the hypocrites in the church. Wisdom from above neutralizes the excuse. Then, in bold and brilliant contrast to a society filled with hypocrisy, the evidence of our transformation and the testimony of our lives can be like Paul's, "by the open statement of the truth we would commend ourselves to everyone's conscience in the sight of God" (2 Corinthians 4:2). As Walter Henrichsen has stated, "When people observe that your life is in harmony with the message, they may not believe, but they know in their conscience that they have met the truth."[12]

Ready to Receive

Think of a setting or relationship in the past when you "wore a mask" of insincerity. What factors contributed to this behavior? Do those factors still prompt your approach to relationships in any way? If so, what key ideas from this chapter will help you toward a wiser sincerity?

Review the descriptions of potential self-deception on pages 182–183. Which of these, if any, has most often been a struggle for you? In light of this, how would you specifically submit this to Christ in the coming weeks to experience his wisdom from above?

Consider again the account of how David's hypocrisy was exposed and resolved by a genuine response to the truth. How will you remain open to the power of truth in your own life? Do you think people in your relational circle feel free to speak truthfully with you about any insincerity in your life? If so, how can you continue to encourage this? If not, look to Christ for the courage to move in this direction for the sake of a truly wise life.

Take time to experience the following Wisdom Prayer, allowing the biblical truths to renew your mind as your prayerful response draws your heart closer to Christ, who is your wisdom.

Wisdom Prayer

Genuine Servants of Christ

We adults spend a significant amount of our lives in the work environment. The New Testament emphasizes sincerity in our work relationships, as we can often be tempted to pretend in order to be well thought of, to get a promotion, or to be sure our work façade is more acceptable than the reality of our life. This temptation also occurs in small groups, PTA meetings, and other networks. With this in mind, let's pray from this passage.

Ephesians 6:5–9

[5] Bondservants, obey your earthly masters with fear and trembling, with a sincere heart, as you would Christ, [6] not by the way of eye-service, as people-pleasers, but as bondservants of Christ, doing the will of God from the heart, [7] rendering service with a good will as to the Lord and not to man, [8] knowing that whatever good anyone does, this he will receive back from the Lord, whether he is a bondservant or is free. [9] Masters, do the same to them, and stop your threatening,

knowing that he who is both their Master and yours is in heaven, and that there is no partiality with him.

REVERENCE—"Who is God?"

Lord Jesus, I praise you because . . .

- You are worthy of my sincere obedience and service (vv. 5, 7)
- You are my divine master, and I am honored to be your bond-servant (v. 6)
- You work in and through my heart to do your will (v. 6)
- You are the rewarder of our good behavior (v. 7)
- You reign in heaven as the Master of all men (v. 9)
- You judge all people impartially (v. 9)

I praise you that you give me a sincere heart to serve you rather than serving ______________________. (vv. 5–6)

I praise you that I can be your bondservant and ultimately serve you alone even when I __________________________. (v. 6)

Thank you that you are a rewarder of good and you will remember my ______________________.

RESPONSE—"How should I respond?"

I confess that I have been a people-pleaser (v. 6) at times, especially when ______________________. Help me to be sincere and serve you only.

REQUESTS—"What should I pray about?"

Give me the wisdom from above that is sincere as I serve you, that I will be a testimony to ______________________ [names].

Help me render service as unto you, and with goodwill, especially as I work with ______________________ [people on the job, at church, volunteer work, etc.].

READINESS—"Where am I headed?"

Because you are my impartial master, give me strength to avoid threatening or coercive behavior when I am tempted to ______________ ______________ [difficult interactions with people].

REVERENCE—"Who is God?"

I praise you that you are a rewarder, so I know it will always be worth it to obey you when ______________________________.

12

Reaping Right Relationships

> And a harvest of righteousness is sown in peace by those who make peace.
>
> James 3:18

> Godly wisdom produces a continuing cycle of righteousness, which is planted and harvested in a peaceful, harmonious relationship between God and his faithful people and between those people themselves.[1]
>
> John MacArthur

It's been said that nothing good grows in the dark. James now pro-vides a summary of one of the interwoven concerns of his letter: that nothing good grows in conflict. Like almond flavoring mixed into cake batter, this truth has been blended into all that James writes about in this letter.

In James 3:18, this church leader and brother of Jesus now gives us an insightful summary of the qualities of wisdom. This verse not only culminates what we have just studied from James 3:13–18 but also transitions into another point of admonitions in chapter 4, where he again addresses the multifaceted environment of conflict.

Sowing and Harvesting

The New American Standard Version of James 3:18 reads, "And the seed whose fruit is righteousness is sown in peace by those who make peace." The literal Amplified Version reads similarly, "And the seed whose fruit is righteousness (spiritual maturity) is sown in peace by those who make peace [by actively encouraging goodwill between individuals]." William Barclay wrote, "We are all trying to reap the harvest which a good life brings. But the seed which brings the rich harvest can never flourish in any atmosphere other than one of right relationships between man and man. And the only people who can sow these seeds and reap the reward are those whose life work it has been to produce such right relationships."[2]

So as we embrace this great summary of the impact of the wisdom of Christ, let's apply some truths about the seed of biblical wisdom, the soil of human hearts and relationships, our role as sowers of this seed, the environment in which the seed grows best, and the amazing harvest we can expect in our lives.

The Power of Seed

The "General Sherman" giant Redwood growing in Sequoia National Park, California, is the largest living thing on Earth. Two hundred seventy-five feet tall, its crown spreads 107 feet. The trunk is more than 26 feet in diameter, taking almost twenty grown men, joining hands, to encircle the base of this massive giant. General Sherman weighs more than 1,000 tons and is over 2,500 years old. John Muir labeled this giant sequoia "the noblest of a noble race." This mammoth specimen of God's creation grew from a seed that was approximately the size of a Rice Krispie. This is one of many illustrations of the incredible power of a seed.

Typically only farmers and gardeners think much about seeds. As one writer noted, "We try to genetically make varieties of oranges that don't have them, we spit them out when we eat watermelons (if they still have them), and we avoid them like the plague if we have diverticulitis."[3] Yet seeds are among the most amazing of God's creation.

The miniscule seed is basically a highly concentrated depository of life-giving DNA. In the right environment, the seed is the essential component of an endless array of living things.

If you are remotely dialed in to nutritional concerns, you know about the value of seeds. TV host Dr. Oz describes seeds as the power plant of nutrition.[4] Sunflower, pumpkin, flax, chia, and hemp seeds are just some of the nutritional treasures that provide concentrated amounts of nutrients, omega-3 fatty acids, antioxidants, minerals, and a variety of essential vitamins.

Most of the food we eat, the materials we use for clothing and furniture, and the supplies that built our homes and provided the furniture all came from seeds. Look outside at the grasses, plants, trees, and creatures of every kind. Over six billion people on this planet—all came from seeds.

The point of this "seed" orientation is to encourage you to think of wisdom as a powerful, supernatural seed. In this passage, "seed represents godly wisdom."[5] Consider the power of the seed of gospel wisdom. It carries mind-boggling capability to conceive and sustain spiritual life. It has the capacity to transform character. The seed of wisdom can grow in order to change relationships, heal marriages, mend families, and make the church of Jesus Christ an authentic and unstoppable force in our broken world.

The Soil

In Mark 4:1–20, Jesus told the striking parable of a sower of seed with the explanation of the implications. The seed of the Word—the truth of gospel wisdom—is sown into hearts. As Jesus explains, some seed is immediately snatched away by our spiritual enemy and never produces results. Some lands on rocky ground. After an initial positive response, difficult times and opposition prove that the seed never really rooted in some people's lives. A third response shows that the soil of the heart allows "the cares of the world and the deceitfulness of riches and the desires for other things enter in" (v. 19) and choke the Word so that it becomes unfruitful. In the final picture of the soil of the heart, Jesus says this person hears the Word, it takes root, and it bears fruit—thirty, sixty, and one hundred times beyond this initial seed.

This is the initial work of our salvation described by Peter: "You have been born again, not of perishable seed but of imperishable, through the living and abiding word of God" (1 Peter 1:23). Now consider the power of the seed of gospel wisdom germinating in a responsive, prayerful, and obedient heart. Like a "General Sherman" of life-giving character, behavior, and relationships, wisdom can truly change one's reality.

Proverbs reminds us in many places of the need to readily receive wisdom in our hearts. The second chapter of Proverbs speaks of an earnest interest toward wisdom. We are challenged to make our "ear attentive to wisdom" and to call out, seeking wisdom like silver and hidden treasure (2:2–4). We are assured that the Lord gives wisdom, storing up in his generous heavenly warehouse its precious and powerful seed for us (2:6–7). The Bible promises the seed of wisdom will "come into your heart . . . and be pleasant to your soul" (2:10). As a result, powerful benefits will bloom—a life of integrity, a deeper fear of the Lord, protection, discretion in relationships, and pure living. One writer notes, "The more wisdom one learns, the more one desires and enjoys it. The protection wisdom gives, moreover, is that it keeps its follower from making decisions that will later bring only regret."[6]

Like many popular worship choruses that speak of giving our heart unreservedly to Christ so that he may speak truth and reign supreme, we must keep our hearts ever open, surrendered and receptive to him and the seed of his life-altering wisdom. As James said earlier in his letter, "Humbly accept the word planted in you, which can save you" (James 1:21 NIV)

The Harvest

James says the seed of wisdom produces the "fruit of righteousness." What is "righteousness"? I love the description offered by one Bible dictionary:

> Righteousness is fulfillment of the expectations in any relationship, whether with God or other people. It is applicable at all levels of society,

> and is relevant in every area of life. Therefore, righteousness denotes the fulfilled expectations in relationships between man and wife, parents and children, fellow citizens, employer and employee, merchant and customers, ruler and citizens, and God and man. Depending on the fulfillment of one's expectations, an individual could be called righteous and his or her acts and speech could be designated as righteous. The opposite of righteous is "evil," "wicked," or "wrong." Righteousness is the fiber which holds society, religion, and family together.[7]

A Chinese proverb says, "If there is righteousness in the heart, there will be beauty in the character. If there is beauty in the character, there will be harmony in the home. If there be harmony in the home, there will be order in the nations. When there is order in the nations, there will be peace in the world." We know Christ ultimately makes these things possible, but the connection between righteousness in the heart as the springboard to well-being at other levels of relationship is spot on.

Only our holy God is ultimately righteous and can provide this righteousness. Psalm 119:137 tells us, "Righteous are you, O Lord, and right are your rules." As one commentator notes, "Not only is God righteous, revealing his righteousness in his mighty acts, but he also expects righteousness of others, who are to reflect the nature of their Creator. The expected response to God's rule is in the form of righteousness, that is, conformity to his rule and will."[8]

Because of sin, none of us is, or can meet, God's required standard of righteousness. As the Bible declares, "None is righteous, no, not one" (Romans 3:10). But the Good News of the gospel tells us that Jesus came to "fulfill all righteousness" (Matthew 3:15). "Jesus is God's final revelation of what he requires of individuals to enter the kingdom and to live righteously. By repentance, faith in Christ, and following the Messiah, each person is again shown how to enter the kingdom."[9]

So by placing one's faith in Christ alone for salvation and righteousness, the Bible tells us that we are "justified." We are made right in the sight of God because of the work of Christ. Speaking about our need for God's grace through Christ, Paul stated, "If righteousness were through the law, then Christ died for no purpose" (Galatians

2:21). Jesus did for us what we could never do by fulfilling God's requirements of right living through his life, death, and resurrection. Yes, this is the great news for wisdom-seekers: "For our sake he made him to be sin who knew no sin, so that in him we might become the righteousness of God" (2 Corinthians 5:21).

So the first prayer for wisdom that God loves to answer is the prayer of placing one's faith in Christ and Christ alone. "The sole condition on which this righteousness is imputed or credited to the believer is faith in or on the Lord Jesus Christ."[10] He then lavishes his saving grace. He cleanses our sin, makes us right with God, gives us a new identity (righteous in his eyes), and makes us a temple of his Holy presence as he imparts divine wisdom and produces right living through us to others. Righteousness is God's plan for every Christ-follower. "If you know that he is righteous, you may be sure that everyone who practices righteousness has been born of him" (1 John 2:29). This fruit of righteousness glorifies God in our words, deeds, and relationships. We are "filled with the fruit of righteousness that comes through Jesus Christ, to the glory and praise of God" (Philippians 1:11).

The Sower

Christ is ultimately the sower who plants his Word and life in us. He also uses human instruments. It may be a pastor who deposits the preached Word in our hearts. We dare not be casual or distracted, checking tweets or dreaming about the afternoon football game on television as the Word is given. We must assume that in the moment of the sermon, God is planting more truth-seeds in our hearts. May the soil be fertile as we listen.

Similarly, a Bible teacher on the radio or an author who exposits truth is a sower of wisdom. With attuned minds and a will to apply God's Word, we can walk the path of greater fruitfulness. When a loving, truth-telling spouse, friend, or work associate offers helpful, hard-to-hear truth, we are benefitted when we consider that possibility that Christ is sowing wisdom into our lives.

He also expects us to cooperate with him in sowing the seed of wisdom into our own submissive hearts. We do this through reading the Word, praying the Scriptures, memorizing Bible passages, and always seeking to apply them like thirsty, drought-stricken soil during a summer rain. Author Michael Griffiths has noted, "We cannot claim ignorance with a dusty unopened Bible on our shelves. We have both the strengthening of the Holy Spirit, making Christ's presence (*and wisdom*) real to us, and what Paul calls the encouragement of the Scriptures (Romans 15:4) to help us."[11] Hosea 10:12 gives a great guideline for our heart cry when we interact with Scripture on a regular basis: "Sow for yourselves righteousness; reap steadfast love; break up your fallow ground, for it is the time to seek the Lord, that he may come and rain righteousness upon you."

To experience the gospel wisdom of Christ in us, Galatians 6:8 says that we are to "sow to the Spirit." In other words, we surrender our mind, will, and energies to the Spirit of Christ in our lives. This produces the fruit or evidence of his life. The fruit basket is composed of "love, joy, peace, patience, kindness, goodness, faithfulness, gentleness, self-control" (Galatians 5:22–23). The promise is that we will "from the Spirit reap eternal life" (Galatians 6:8).

And here is an even more specific description of the wise sower. We are described as sowers who "make peace" (James 3:18). Picture someone seeking to plant a garden by blasting a shotgun into the ground or whacking away angrily at the dirt with an axe. Imagine someone in a garden, carelessly throwing seed in a rage to any and every direction with no concern for the quantity, the destination, or the result. Foolish indeed.

Now imagine a gardener—relaxed, patient, enjoying the moment. She carefully prepares the soil. She attentively selects the seed. With serene sensitivity she waters, fertilizes, and removes weeds.

Which gardener should have the expectation of a healthy harvest? Cleary the one who sows in peace will see fruit. Again, under the rule of Christ, who is the peaceable wisdom from above, we daily and moment-by-moment sow the seeds of gospel wisdom. We expect a crop of righteousness. Commenting on this, John MacArthur says, "It is possible that James had in mind the idea of fruit being harvested and then, in part, becoming seed, which is re-sown in peace, as it were, and produces still more fruit, and so on, in the familiar cycle of growing and reaping."[12]

The Environment

So when we make peace, not war, the environment changes and provides a healthy atmosphere for the fruit of righteousness. James tells us that the seed of wisdom that produces righteousness is sown in an environment of peace.

Environment matters. Because of the nature of my pastoral calling and my entrepreneurial wiring, our family has lived in the rain of the Pacific Northwest, the sunshine of California, the frozen winters of Minnesota, the humid summers of central Virginia, and the high and dry altitudes of Colorado. In each location we have enjoyed gardening. But before we got carried away planting our favorite flowers or annuals, we needed to see what would flourish in each particular zone. Some plants explode with life in one environment but end in a shriveled death in the same environment.

Environment is huge in society. Avid environmentalists advocate against modern advancements that may negatively affect our global ecosystem. Their intentions are fueled by a desire that life on this planet in its most natural form must be protected from the intrusions of human enterprise. An entire government agency, the Environmental Protection Agency, monitors, negotiates, and regulates these debates.

We work hard to create a positive work environment. We invest money, time, and great care to design a comfortable home environment. Churches even give great attention and funding to create a "worship environment" that they think will attract newcomers and enhance the enjoyment factor in weekend services.

The environment that produces a harvest of right living is summed up in one word: peace. Fruitful wisdom is sown in peace by a peacemaker.

James regularly spoke of the counterproductive environment of conflict in light of the call to live rightly: "For the anger of man does not produce the righteousness of God" (James 1:20). In chapter 3, he taught extensively on the "fire," "restless evil," and "deadly poison" of an untamed tongue (vv. 1–12). He denounced "jealousy and selfish ambition" that was producing "disorder and every vile practice" (vv. 14–16). In James 4:1–4, he speaks of quarrels and fights that result from a heart that loves the world more than God. He again confronts their evil speech toward one another (4:11–12). Finally, James condemns the rich who are promoting injustice and conflict by cheating their employees (5:1–6). These were believers in great need of peace.

But James confronts discord with full confidence that hearts, relationships, families, congregations, and communities can be transformed. James commands only what he knows Christ is sufficient to provide. Peace is possible and righteousness is reassured because of Jesus Christ, our wisdom from above.

Keys to the Harvest

My earnest prayer is that the impact of this book is going to produce a lasting, life-changing, relationship-restoring, gospel-worthy, Christ-glorifying harvest in your life. With that in mind, let me close this chapter with a few final thoughts for your encouragement.

It Takes Work

I've known some farmers over the years. They were all hard workers. The land seldom took a recess. Beyond the relentless care demanded by the plowing, planting, watering, and harvesting, there were always unpredictable threats. Weather, disease, and invasive insects were just a few.

Applying the wisdom of the New Testament is possible only because we have the mind of Christ who is our indwelling source of wisdom (1 Corinthians 1:30; 2:16). In parallel, the New Testament says, "The righteous shall live by faith" (Romans 1:17; Galatians 3:11; Hebrews 10:38). So the work of faith is essential for the harvest of righteousness in marriage, parenting, and other relationships.

Like the farmer desiring a harvest, we must be attentive and diligent to the process of righteous living in our interactions. "Have this mind among yourselves," Paul taught in Philippians 2. Then he went on to speak of the responsibility of the church to be blameless, innocent, and fruitful as we "shine as lights" and "hold fast to the word of life" in the midst of a "crooked and twisted generation." To do this fruitfully, he says we must "work out" our own salvation with fear and trembling: "For it is God who works in you, both to will and to do for his good pleasure" (vv. 12–15).

So Christ is sufficient to manifest wisdom in and through us. But we must work out these realities. Paul is not just talking about the individual efforts. Rather, he is speaking to the church as they model the mind of Christ that he just described.

To state the obvious, relationships take work. I have often said that marriage is God's ultimate character development tool. Every relationship is dynamic because it involves two or more imperfect people aiming for a perfect standard, indwelt by a perfect Christ but embracing a very flawed and fickle obedience. "It is this 'long obedience in the same direction' which the mood of the world does so much to discourage."[13]

It Takes Time

We've all known the tests of patience when waiting for the desire of our hearts, whether it is the completion of a house project, the arrival of a special gift in the mail, the ripening of fruit on a backyard tree, the birth of a baby, or the maturing of that child to a responsible, self-sufficient adult. Sowing and harvesting take time. Transforming a relationship takes months, sometimes years. Allowing Christ to change your own habits of reaction, emotion, and speech can feel like two steps forward and three steps back.

But take heart, persevere, and trust God for the fruit of wisdom in your life. Admittedly, we are not good at assessing the slow processes of our own growth. Sometimes we can feel like a twelve-year-old who must have marks on the wall to measure our height year by year. The marks make our progress obvious even though we know we are always growing. Our "markers on the wall" might be the feedback from a friend, personal journal entries that show objective progress, or the "fruit" of obvious change observed by a spouse. In any case, we know God is faithful as we walk by faith. He loves to answer our prayers for gospel wisdom.

James wrote earlier in his letter, "Make sure that your endurance carries you all the way without failing, so that you may be perfect and complete, lacking nothing" (1:4 GNT). Then, in the following verses he compels us to ask in faith for wisdom from above, without wavering. Again, the needful reminder is that God gives this wisdom generously and without reproach.

By his own promise, God is a faithful rewarder of those who diligently seek him (Hebrews 11:6). Proverbs 11:18 affirms, "One who sows righteousness gets a sure reward." Like reassuring worship songs playing in the car on a long drive, we have this promise: "The effect of righteousness will be peace, and the result of righteousness, quietness and trust forever" (Isaiah 32:17).

It Takes God!

Yes, we sow, wait, work, and eventually reap a harvest. We do so in great hope because we have a great Christ. We are not grunting hard, sweating and shaking, trying to force the emergence of the fruit of righteousness based on some misinformed self-confidence. As Paul said, his longing was to "be found in him, not having a righteousness of my own that comes from the law, but that which comes through faith in Christ, the righteousness from God that depends on faith" (Philippians 3:9).

Remember our description of righteousness earlier?

> Righteousness denotes the fulfilled expectations in relationships between man and wife, parents and children, fellow citizens, employer and employee, merchant and customers, ruler and citizens, and God and man. . . . Righteousness is the fiber which holds society, religion, and family together.

The triune God—Father, Son, and Holy Spirit—living eternally in perfect relationship is fully committed to your righteousness. He fulfilled it in the work of the cross. He is fulfilling it through his power in you. "He who calls you is faithful; he will surely do it" (1 Thessalonians 5:24). It is his character to give the seed of wisdom generously. We must ask. It is indeed a prayer he loves to answer. His answers will allow us to sow in peace and reap an abundant harvest. So let us sow in great confidence and hope because "he who supplies seed to the sower and bread for food will supply and multiply your seed for sowing and increase the harvest of your righteousness" (2 Corinthians 9:10). Amen and amen!

Ready to Receive

This chapter speaks of the environment of right relationships. As you look back over the past few years, what kind of environment have you cultivated at home, work, church, and elsewhere? How has this study prompted you to improve that environment? Write down a few specific areas needing improvement.

As you have read of the need to receive the truth of God's Word in the soil of a humble heart in order to exhibit a life of righteousness, think of two or three commitments that will help you stay in that posture during the course of an average week. When and where you will seek to practice these disciplines? Ask Christ for grace and resolve to keep these commitments as a matter of your lifestyle.

You've just read that the harvest of gospel wisdom takes work, time, and God. As you complete this study, how will you continue to submit to the Spirit of Christ on a moment-by-moment basis for the rest of your life? Think of the specific relationships that will require this effort. Now meditate for a few minutes on the closing promise from 2 Corinthians 9:10. Thank the Lord Jesus for his pledge to fulfill this promise in and through you.

Take time to experience the following Wisdom Prayer, allowing the biblical truths to renew your mind as your prayerful response draws your heart closer to Christ, who is your wisdom.

Wisdom Prayer

Bearing Righteous Fruit

Paul had a deep affection for the Christians at Philippi because of their supportive partnership with Paul in the gospel. As he writes from prison, he prays for them. In the early part of his letter he shared his confidence that what Christ had begun in them, he would complete (Philippians 1:6). With this in mind, he prays for them to exhibit the fruit of righteousness. This prayer will be the springboard to our prayer.

Philippians 1:9–11

9 It is my prayer that your love may abound more and more, with
knowledge and all discernment, 10 so that you may approve what is
excellent, and so be pure and blameless for the day of Christ, 11 filled
with the fruit of righteousness that comes through Jesus Christ, to
the glory and praise of God.

REVERENCE—"Who is God?"

Lord Jesus, I praise you because . . .

- Your love fills our hearts and abounds more and more (v. 9)
- You have drawn me to a deep experiential knowledge of you (v. 9)
- You have given me your moral discretion/discernment (v. 9)
- You empower me for spiritual excellence—knowing and doing the best things (v. 10)
- You are purifying me and producing blamelessness in me (v. 10)
- I have the sure hope of the "day of Christ" when I will see you face to face (v. 10)
- You produce and fill me with your righteousness (v. 11)
- You work in my life to bring glory to God (v. 11)

Lord Jesus, I praise you for your self-sacrificing love for me that empowers me to continue to grow in love for ______________________ [names]. (v. 9)

Lord Jesus, I praise you that you have given me a real, experiential knowledge that you are ____________________________ [characteristic of Christ]. I want to know you more.

Thank you that even though this world is ________________________, you give me moral discernment to know your will.

RESPONSE—"How should I respond?"

I confess that I need special grace to abound in love toward ________ ______________ [names].

I confess that rather than aiming for excellence (the best things), I have often settled for less in _______________________ [an area of your life].

REQUESTS—"What should I pray about?"

Lord Jesus, produce in me the fruit of your righteousness . . .

- In my relationship with _______________________ [names].
- As I am facing the challenge of _________________________ .
- In my personal struggle with ____________________________.

READINESS—"Where am I headed?"

As I live in a world filled with compromise, give me your wisdom to be pure and blameless, especially when ____________________________.

REVERENCE—"Who is God?"

I praise you that my growth in righteousness is ultimately for your glory. So this week be glorified as I ______________________________.

Conclusion

Daily Delight and Dependence

Wisdom is God-given orientation that has profound practical effects on the way a person lives. Like true faith, true wisdom is identified by the quality of life that it produces.[1]

Douglas Moo

O God, the Eternal All, help me to know that
All things are shadow, but thou are substance,
All things are quicksand, but thou art mountain,
All things are shifting, but thou art anchor,
All things are ignorance, but thou art wisdom.[2]

A Puritan Prayer

In his excellent devotional *Thoughts From the Diary of a Desperate Man*, Walter Henrichsen writes of the biblical priority of relationships. In doing so he describes five kinds of relationships:

1. A Christian with a Christian with Christ at the center.
2. A Christian with a non-Christian with Christ at the center.
3. A non-Christian with a non-Christian.

4. A Christian with a Christian when Christ isn't central.
5. A Christian with a non-Christian where Christ isn't central.

Henrichsen concludes that the object of the first relationship is edification and the second evangelism. He further observes that the Bible does not deal with relationships three through five, since it knows nothing of people relating to one another with no thought of God, stating, "The only valid relationships you have in life are those where Christ is the center—not business, and not sports."[3]

Then, Henrichsen makes this observation:

> You learn to glorify God by how you relate to others. . . . All relationships have as their goal either the person coming into a saving relationship with Jesus or the person growing in his love and commitment to the Savior. If your relationship with others does not center on evangelism and edification, you are acting contrary to God's intent for your life.[4]

Give Us This Day our Daily Mission

God grants us breath each day so that we might live for his glory through relationships that result in either edification of the saved or evangelism of the lost. This is only possible by the wisdom of Jesus. Accomplishing this on a daily basis truly satisfies our deepest need for mission and meaning.

I've said it often and over many years that the hardest thing about the Christian life is that it is so *daily*. Mission and meaning, passion and purpose, are very daily. Paul affirms the reality of this dynamic of the Christian journey when he says, "So we do not lose heart. Though our outer self is wasting away, our inner self is being renewed *day by day*" (2 Corinthians 4:16). In Proverbs 8:34, wisdom makes this appeal, "Blessed is the one who listens to me, watching *daily* at my gates, waiting beside my doors." Our quest for wisdom is achieved or squandered in daily increments.

The application of gospel wisdom will fall short if it culminates in the reshelving or resale of a book you've just completed. This wisdom will not be real if it is reduced to a few pithy ideas that are tucked away in your memory bank. Yes, memorizing the biblical text of James 3:17–18 will provide the potential of powerful renewal, as has been the case in my life. But in the long run, apart from relentless and renewing daily application of New Testament wisdom, we will abort the potential of this vital ingredient for Christ-honoring character and contribution.

Paul's words in 2 Corinthians 4:16 (above) assure us of three things:

We can experience authentic encouragement every day. I define discouragement as a temporary loss of perspective. Daily renewal in the principles of gospel wisdom can empower us to keep perspective based on truth, leading to transformation and triumph. When your marriage gets messy, your colleagues are combative, and raising your children gets complicated, do not lose heart. Remember, as Paul did, that "we have this treasure in jars of clay, to show that the surpassing power belongs to God and not to us" (2 Corinthians 4:7). You may not be able to "figure it out" in the perplexing moments of life, but you can resolve to follow him. You may fail miserably one day, but the next day is the dawn of new opportunity. Christ, the wisdom of God, will lead you and live in you, resulting in a growing fulfillment of his mission and your sense of meaning.

Every day we are closer to the finish line of our lives. The "vapor" of our physical existence (as James described it in James 4:14) should instill new intensity and intentionality in our focus on the things that really matter during this brief earthly appearance. Every day matters in light of a fast-approaching eternal reward. On that day we will give an account for our stewardship of edification and evangelism through our relationships.

The battle for purpose and perspective can result in victory with every sunrise and sunset as the "inner self is being renewed day by day." This renewal through the memorization, meditation, and prayerful application of the truth of gospel wisdom is the necessary pursuit for daily fulfillment and fruitfulness.

My prayer for my own heart and yours is that every day we keep the realities of wisdom ever in reach and at the forefront of our lives. Given all the unpredictable circumstances, demanding challenges, and difficult relationships that factor into each day, may we live with the confidence that we can truly exhibit the wisdom from above that is "first pure, then peaceable, gentle, open to reason, full of mercy and good fruits, impartial and sincere." The fruit of right living can be the testimony of our lives both in our influence on other believers and our authentic witness to the lost.

Coming full circle, we must delight in the all-wise, ever-indwelling, and ultimately sufficient Christ each day. As we think of him, we can be specific in the application of his life through these New Testament descriptions of practical wisdom. Flowing from this delight, we can consistently express a humble dependence on him through unceasing prayer—confident that he loves to answer.

As we close, I offer a prayer for gospel wisdom that I trust will represent the cry of your heart and the hope for every relationship in your life. While you might not articulate a word-for-word expression of this prayer, I hope you will make it a heart-to-heart expression of his worth and your need for the wisdom that comes generously from above.

A Prayer for Gospel Wisdom—
One That God Loves to Answer

Lord Jesus Christ, you are wisdom, living in me, so I trust you to make me . . .

Pure—*Because you are the spotless Lamb of God, without sin. When lust, selfish ambition, and jealousy assail my heart, I will invite you to rule in me by your triumphant and holy presence.*

Peaceable—*Because you are the Prince of Peace and your peace overcomes the world. When my bent toward anger, conflict, and control produces turmoil, I will submit to your full provision of peace that passes all understanding.*

Gentle—*Because you are the Gentle Shepherd and humble and gentle at heart. When my words are hurtful and my attitudes are harsh, I will humble myself and trust you to make me strong enough to be meek like you.*

Open to reason—*Because you willingly yielded to the Father's plan to give your life for me. When I am driven to win every argument and dominate others with my views, I will surrender* *to your desire that I would be teachable, willing to change, and ready to forgive.*

Full of mercy—*Because you delight in mercy and demonstrated great mercy toward sinners. When I am feeling superior, judgmental, and hard-hearted, I will remember your abundant mercy to me and open my heart to your mercy through me.*

Full of good fruits—*Because you have begun a good work in me and I am your workmanship created by you for good works. When I lose focus on the good fruits you desire to display to others, I will worship your goodness and prayerfully yield to your good Spirit in me.*

Wisdom is Jesus Christ—embraced, experienced, exemplified, and exalted in our lives and relationships.

Impartial—*Because you are a friend of sinners and lover of all souls. When I see people through carnal eyes and try to use them for my selfish purposes, I will kneel before the One who loves and cares for all persons without prejudice.*

Sincere—*Because you are the truth and all your words and works are true. When I believe, receive, and relish anything other than the truth, I will invite you to confront my hypocrisy and bring me to fresh repentance according to your Word.*

Produce in and through me the peaceable fruit of righteousness for your glory and for the good of all those with whom you have placed me in relationship and for your glory.

Amen.

Acknowledgments

Writing projects like this are always a team effort, even though only one name appears on the book spine. Knowing this, I want to express my genuine thanks.

First, to Rosemary. Your decades of loving support and patient endurance have kept me in the game—especially when I had a writing deadline. Thank you for your understanding, prayers, and grace that are not always acknowledged on earth but will be greatly rewarded in heaven. I am blessed to have you as my wife.

To my staff at Strategic Renewal and The 6:4 Fellowship for graciously picking up the slack on those many days when I was buried in the creative process of producing a book. You are a great team, and I am grateful for how each of you complements my leadership and passionately supports our mission.

To the board of Strategic Renewal as you have continued to provide guidance, accountability, and prayer support for our ministry. Thanks for cheering me on over these many months.

To my ministry prayer partners who faithfully express love on their knees in intercession for my family, ministry and, specifically, this writing project.

To Sid and Carol and Ed and Janeen for providing a quiet and beautiful space to experience the Creator and write without distraction.

To Andy McGuire, Jeff Braun, and the team at Bethany House for continuing to encourage my writing efforts and believing in this third project together.

Appendix 1

Jesus' Model of Prayer

The Wisdom Prayers at the end of each chapter are intended to provide a very easy, memorable, and applicable tool you can you use at any time to apply the truths of the chapter through a time of prayer.

Simple and Applicable

In the mid-1990s I discovered a very simple way to understand and implement the model prayer found in Matthew 6:9–13 (also known as the Lord's Prayer). I call it the "For Dummies" version because is it so simple and immediately applicable—and memorable. It has become a standard approach for my personal prayers. Every time I look at a biblical text as a springboard to prayer, I think in terms of this pattern. It is almost as if this diagram is engraved on my bifocals.

I have also taught this pattern to thousands of pastors, prayer leaders, and church members. In my book *Transforming Prayer* (Bethany House), I explain in depth how to use this approach in praying from virtually any passage of Scripture. Here, we will use this pattern to spark a worship-based approach in seeking God's face, then trusting him for the vital issues of your journey as we seek to apply gospel wisdom.

The Profound Made Simple

I grew up with a love for music. I played a couple instruments, sang in high school all-state choirs, and received a scholarship for vocal music for two of my four years of college. So it was natural that I experienced a convergence between my love for the Lord's Prayer and my love for music. The result is what I call the 4/4 Pattern of Prayer.

In music, the 4/4 pattern is the most basic beat. In adapting the elements of that pattern to the Lord's Prayer, it looks like this:

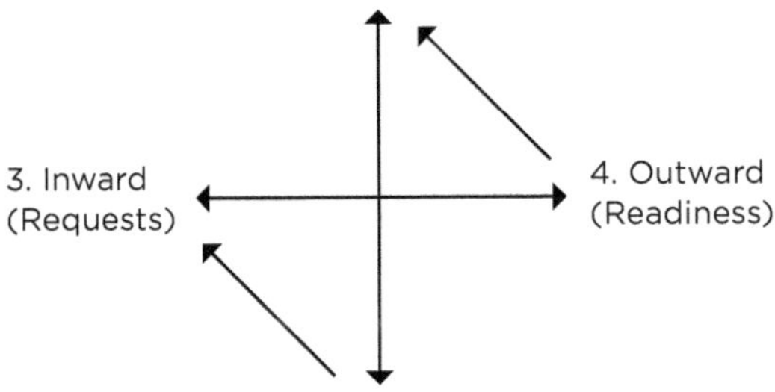

As you think about this pattern, keep in mind that our prayers begin in the Scriptures, so I always start with an open Bible. Very often I use a psalm. In this book we focus on some key passages related to Christ and the theme of wisdom. We also know that our teacher is the Holy Spirit. We come to the text with a ready mind, but also with our entire being completely surrendered to the instruction of the Holy Spirit as we pray.

▲ The Starting Place: Reverence (The Question: Who Is God?)

Imagine a conductor before an orchestra. The conductor raises a hand high to capture the attention of the musicians. Every member is at full attention. In the prayer pattern Jesus gave his disciples, he instructs us to begin with this upward focus of worship ("Our Father in heaven, hallowed be your name"). We call this upward focus or *reverence*. In keeping with Jesus' instructions, prayer begins with the character of God as we take time to focus our entire beings on the wonders of who God is.

As our Father, he is caring and intimate. As the One who is in heaven, he is transcendent, holy, and separate. His holy name points us to his matchless character.

One writer says that this focus "calls for us to think about God, and in particular his name. Our prayers are to be suffused with large thoughts about God. We are to take the attributes of God, which are suggested by his various names. If our prayers are not focused on God we are guilty of 'idolatry' as we are putting someone (or something) else in God's place."[1]

Spending quality time with an open Bible, delighting in the names and character of God, is the most important engagement in our lives and the vital starting point of prayer. We essentially ask the question, "What does this passage show me about God and his character? How can I worship him based on these truths?" This rivets our entire being on his name and sets our hearts on his glory as the goal of all prayer. It allows us to abide in him as his word abides in us, and brings us into conformity to the Lord Jesus so that we truly pray "in his name."

Not only is our *reverence* a springboard to intimate, biblical, extended worship, but it is vital to the exercise of real faith in prayer. Hebrews 11:6 says, "Without faith it is impossible to please him, for whoever would draw near to God must believe that he exists and that he rewards those who seek him." Consider that all our praying may not please God if we do not pray in the faith that comes from the Word of God (Romans 10:17). This "upward" start puts our hearts in full attention and awe of who God is, and assures us of his character and commitment to reward us as we set our hearts to seek *him*, not just things *from* him.

▾ The Downward Stroke: Response (The Question: How Should I Respond?)

Next, the musical conductor gives the downbeat and the composition begins. In this prayer pattern, our "music" of worship and praise has already commenced. Now we *respond* to God's character. Jesus taught the essence of this when he said, "Your kingdom come. Your will be done on earth as it is in heaven." This *response* to God's character in prayer involves yielding to the control of the Holy Spirit and recommitting to God's kingdom purposes. I often note that worship is the response of all I am to the revelation of all he is. Introspection and surrender mark this time of yielding to the Spirit's promptings. It is a season of pledged obedience to the will and Word of God, desiring the accomplishment of his purposes in our lives.

Scottish writer Robert Law said, "Prayer is a mighty instrument, not for getting man's will done in heaven, but for getting God's will done on earth."[2] Warren Wiersbe explains that this moment of prayer involves "the devotion and dedication of our entire being to Jesus as we eagerly anticipate seeing him."[3] It involves praying with the obedience and surrender to Jesus who said, "Not My will, but Yours be done" (Luke 22:42 NASB) for the sake of the Father's glory and kingdom purposes.

◂ The Inward Stroke: Requests (The Question: What Should I Pray About?)

From the downbeat, the conductor now moves the baton, slanting upward and left, setting the tempo for the music. In prayer, we are now ready to express trust in God for the needs of our lives by way of our *requests*. I often say that we do not really know what to ask for until we have worshiped well and surrendered completely. Psalm 9:10 says, "Those who know your name will put their trust in you." From this position of spiritual alignment, we come to the Father with our requests.

"Give us this day our daily bread, and forgive us our debts, as we forgive our debtors" invites us to pray about the *resource* and *relationship* issues of life. If we looked at the average prayer list, virtually every request would ultimately be a resource concern or a relationship concern. Jesus, in his divine wisdom, knew our journey and our struggles. This segment of trusting him with a variety of "inward" matters allows us to lay it all out before him.

Praying about "daily bread" is more than hoping we can scrape some funds together to buy a fresh bagel at Panera. This idea represents "all that we need to sustain life as we serve the Lord."[4] This is not a time of informing God of our needs, because he knows what we need before we ask (Matthew 6:8). Rather, this is an expression of conscious trust in God as the perfect definer and provider of our needs. It involves prayer about personal concerns, family and friends, daily circumstances, and even ministry matters.

Relationships matter to God. As the word and Spirit are working in us, leading us into prayer "according to the will of God" (Romans 8:27), we will be compelled to evaluate our relationships to be sure that our conscience is clear and relationships are right (Acts 24:16).

We come to a place of relational alignment in this moment of prayer. This requires our confession of any sin that is revealed, leading to confession and restoration—both vertically (with the Lord) and horizontally (with others). Christians are a forgiven and forgiving people. This element of the prayer addresses the inward realities of our heart to align us with the heart of the One who is the God of self-sacrificing, gracious, merciful, and forgiving love.

▸ The Outward Stroke: Readiness (The Question: Where Am I Going?)

As the music continues, the conductor moves the beat to the right, keeping tempo. As our prayer continues, the outward stroke reminds us that we are going into a spiritual contest. It's a war zone out there. More importantly, this moment of prayer reassures us of the spiritual resources within us. We know the time comes when we must get off or knees and re-enter the spiritual contest. We must be battle *ready*.

When we pray, "Do not lead us into temptation, but deliver us from the evil one," we recognize our own inability to overcome the temptations and snares of daily life. We entrust our welfare for the warfare to the one who is our victor. Borrowing from the great spiritual combat text of Ephesians 6:10–20, we prepare our hearts and minds to "be strong in the Lord and in the power of his might" as we "put on the whole armor of God . . . to stand against the schemes of the devil" (vv. 10–11). In this moment of *readiness* for the battle, we affirm that "we do not wrestle against flesh and blood, but against the rulers, against the authorities, against the cosmic powers over this present darkness, against the spiritual forces of evil in the heavenly places" (v. 12).

We are praying to be battle *ready* through our trust in Christ. He is able to "provide the way of escape" (1 Corinthians 10:13) and his Word is sufficient to equip us in the face of any temptation (see the example of Jesus in Matthew 4:2–11).

As we come to the concluding moments of a prayer time, we not only anticipate but also embrace the responsibility to fight the good fight. We are called to be praying menaces to the devil. Prayer is not an escape from the battles of life but a great equipping to fight them in supernatural power. The very fact that we are seeking God's face and engaging in life-giving prayer alerts the enemy to our increased threat to his dominion. When we pray, we pick a fight with the devil at a completely new level. Yet this is why we are on earth—not to cruise along on a luxury liner until Jesus comes, but to stay actively engaged in our "search and rescue mission" in the midst of the global spiritual battle for the hearts and minds of people.

▲ The Upward Stroke: Reverence (The Question: Who Is God?)

With an upward motion, the conductor returns the beat to the starting point. The traditional version we recite (from the King James Version of Matthew 6:13), concludes on a high note of praise: "For thine is the kingdom, and the power, and the glory, for ever. Amen." We conclude our prayer with a "doxology," which is an expression giving glory to God. We close the door on prayer the same way we opened it—with praise.

Appendix 2

New Testament Descriptions of Gospel Relationships

While these comparisons are not exact and, in some instances, represent similarities, this does give us a sense of things that matter most in our relationships from a New Testament perspective.

The Wisdom from Above (James 3:17–18)	**The Beatitudes** (Matthew 5:2–12)	**The Marks of Genuine Love** (1 Corinthians 13:1–8)	**The Fruit of the Holy Spirit** (Galatians 5:22–23)
Context: Contrasting wisdom from above with wisdom from below that produces relational conflict	**Context:** The blessings and character of those who are part of God's kingdom through Christ	**Context:** Correction to the confused and self-edifying use of spiritual gifts	**Context:** Contrasting the destructive works of the flesh with the evidence of the Spirit's life
First pure	Blessed are the pure in heart	It does not rejoice at wrongdoing, but rejoices with the truth	Self-control

The Wisdom from Above (James 3:17–18)	**The Beatitudes** (Matthew 5:2–12)	**The Marks of Genuine Love** (1 Corinthians 13:1–8)	**The Fruit of the Holy Spirit** (Galatians 5:22–23)
Peaceable	Blessed are the peacemakers	Patient	Peace
Gentle	Blessed are those who are persecuted for righteousness' sake	Kind	Gentleness
Open to reason	Blessed are the poor in spirit	Love does not envy or boast; it is not arrogant or rude	Kindness
Full of mercy	Blessed are the merciful	It is not irritable or resentful	Patience
Full of good fruits	Blessed are those who hunger and thirst for righteousness	Love bears all things, believes all things, hopes all things, endures all things	Goodness
Impartial	Blessed are you when others revile you . . . and utter all kinds of evil against you falsely on my account. Rejoice and be glad.	It does not insist on its own way	Love
Sincere	Jesus confronted hypocrisy four times in the Sermon on the Mount (6:2,5,17;7:5)	Never ends	Faithfulness

All this is made possible through the gospel, is primarily relational, and is manifested through Christ living in us.

Application and Discussion Questions

Chapter 1—Wise Beyond Solomon

1. Read the account of Solomon's moral slide and the eventual consequences in 1 Kings 11:1–43. In spite of God's blessings (see a quick example in 1 Kings 10:23–25), Solomon failed relationally. As you read this chapter, identify how he stumbled in his relationship with God. How did he fail maritally? How did he fail with his son? Why do we need the grace of Christ to avoid the same pathway of destruction today?
2. Read the account of the early days of Rehoboam, Solomon's son, in 1 Kings 12:1–15. What do you think guided his approach to relationships? Where did he get this set of values? Does the world still allure us to these kinds of values today? If so, how? Look at 1 John 2:15–17. What command are we given here and why? What promise can you embrace today from this passage?
3. Read Matthew 12:38–42. Notice especially the reference to the Queen of the South and Solomon. How did she express a hunger for the wisdom of Solomon? How were the people of Jesus' day failing to demonstrate an interest in the wisdom of Jesus? How are you demonstrating a hunger for the wisdom of Jesus

today? What would indicate your hunger and sacrifice to gain that wisdom?

Chapter 2—Accessing Your Wisdom Treasure

1. Read James 1:5–8. When we feel the need for wisdom, what does James tell us we must do? What is it about God's character that compels us to ask in faith? From your understanding of the Scriptures and based on your experience of walking with God, how have you seen evidences of his generous character?
2. God is generous in giving his wisdom to us. What do we know about the magnitude of the wisdom of God from Romans 11:33–36? How much wisdom does he have to give? See another description of the wisdom resources found in Christ (see Colossians 1: 9–10). Now, how does this strengthen your faith as you pray for wisdom?
3. Read 1 Corinthians 1:20–31. How is the wisdom of the world described? Why is it inadequate? What is the source of the wisdom of God? How is it effective to, in, and through us? What should be our response to this provision of gospel wisdom?

Chapter 3—The Relational Game Changer

1. Review the relational failure of this world's wisdom (see 1 Corinthians 3:18–21). Now read the story behind these conclusions in 3:1–17. How does worldly wisdom undermine relationships? Has there been a time in your life when you experienced the negative impact of earthly wisdom in your relationships? How did you—or how can you—find a new path for relationally positive wisdom?
2. Take some time to look at the chart in appendix 2. This shows similarities in some of the great lists of Christian virtues. Now think about your network of relationships. Try to write the name of someone you feel you need to relate to more authentically in connection with the description in each of thirty-six boxes.

(Some names might be noted multiple times.) Now ask God for wisdom from above to act upon those promptings in the coming weeks.

3. In this chapter we reviewed the authenticity of the relationship of Jesus and the Father (from John 1). Jesus demonstrated divine wisdom in his earthly relationships throughout his ministry. Now review a few glimpses of Jesus' final moments with his inner circle in John 13:1–17, 31–34, and 14:12–17. Make a list of the words that describe his relational wisdom. Which of these do you need to ask for more faithfully in anticipation of God's answer to transform your relationships?

Chapter 4—Purely Wise in a Wicked World

1. The wisdom from above is pure because God is pure and holy. The risen Christ is glorious and righteous (compare Isaiah 6:1–8 with Revelation 1:12–18 and Revelation 5:6–14). What similarities do you find? How would you describe, in your own words, these scenes of holiness? How does it make you feel to realize that the very presence of the Holy One lives in you? How does this motivate you to ask for the wisdom from above that is first pure?
2. Wisdom from above compels us to live with pure motives. When in the past did you appear to do the right thing only to realize you had the wrong motives? How did you come to this realization? Now review some verses that reveal the motives of Jesus (see Mark 10:35; John 4:24; 5:19; and 17:4, 6). How does the example of Jesus compel you to ask for his wisdom for a purer motivation?
3. The book of Proverbs often contrasts the purity that flows from wisdom with the destructive impurity that results from rejecting wisdom. One such section is Proverbs 4:1–27. As you read, compile a list of the benefits of wisdom. Likewise, note the negative consequences of rejecting wisdom. Now think of the character of Jesus and how you can trust him to help you apply this wisdom.

Chapter 5—Wisdom Wins in a Culture at War

1. Puritan Thomas Watson summarized, "The Father is called the 'God of Peace' (Hebrews 13:20). The Son is called the 'Prince of Peace' (Isaiah 9:6). The Holy Spirit is the Spirit of Peace (Ephesians 4:3). The more a person is peaceable, the more he is like God. . . . Those born of God are peacemakers."[1] Even though your core identity is that of a peacemaker, when, in the course of a normal week, are you most prone to violate that identity? Why? How would the promise of Isaiah 26:3 help you with your thoughts in times like this?
2. First Timothy 2:1–2 and Philippians 4:6–7 both make a connection between peace and prayer. Why do you think this is the case? What happens in our souls when we pray? When have you experienced this connection most clearly in recent weeks?
3. In John 14:27, Jesus gave a promise of peace. He also contrasted it to the peace that the world gives. How does the world promise a superficial and temporary peace? How are people trying to find that peace? Why is Jesus able to give a greater and deeper sense of peace according to this verse?

Chapter 6—Gentle Wisdom—Still in Style

1. Read Proverbs 15:1. When have you found this principle to be true in your own experience? Have you ever violated this principle? What was the result? Considering the relationships in your life today, when do you think you might have an occasion to put this into practice in the near future?
2. Notice the picture of gentleness given in 1 Thessalonians 2:7. What kind of ministry would a person have if he or she adopted this attitude? How is this the way you minister to your children? Your spouse? Fellow believers? How might you improve the gentleness factor in your ministry?
3. Notice the admonitions of 1 Peter 3:3–5 and 3:7. How is gentleness profitable in marriage on the part of both husband and

wife? What dynamics tend to undermine this gentle behavior? What benefits can you expect by complying with these practices of gentleness?

Chapter 7—Wise Reason for Unreasonable People

1. Read Matthew 18:21–35. In what way was this servant unreasonable with people? How do people today display this same kind of unreasonable behavior? What truths should this servant have understood to be more reasonable?
2. James 1:19–21 is a call to reason. How so? What are the negative effects of a lack of submission and yieldedness? What prescription is given to help us with a more reasonable approach? How would this help?
3. To be reasonable implies a willingness to yield, submit, and change. Read James 4:13–17. In what ways do the attitudes described here violate the reasonableness of wisdom? Does this provide an insight for your struggles to yield your will? If so, how?

Chapter 8—Mercy Me, I'm Getting Wiser!

1. Look up Psalm 41:1 along with Proverbs 11:17, 14:21, and 19:17. How do these describe an expression of mercy? What benefits are promised for the merciful? How can you put this into practice in the next week?
2. Isaiah chapter 58 describes Old Testament Israel's ritual of fasting. But in confronting their superficial approach, God calls them to display the true heart of fasting by showing mercy. How would this mercy be evidenced? How do we sometimes get so busy with church work that, like these Israelites, we fail to show mercy? What promises are given here for the merciful?
3. Jesus elevated mercy in the Parable of the Good Samaritan. Read this familiar story in Luke 10:25–37. What kept the first two passersby from showing mercy? Do you ever manifest similar

behavior? What opportunities might you have in the coming week to follow the model of the Good Samaritan? In connection with what Jesus said in vv. 27–28, why is mercy important?

Chapter 9—How the Good Die Wise

1. Consider Colossians 1:9–12, where Paul prays for us to bear fruit in every good work. What other elements of a godly life are in this context? How do these also represent a life full of good works? What is the source of these good works? How can you apply this to your Christian walk this week?
2. Read Acts 11:22–26, where Barnabas is described as a man who was good. What clues do we find here about his good and fruitful life? How might the Lord want to produce these same evidences of goodness through you? What might it look like in your family, work, or church involvement?
3. John 15:1–5 gives a powerful illustration of how we might produce good fruit. What is our source of this fruit? How can you diligently practice this each day? What good fruits do you trust the Lord to produce in you this week in your work or ministry? Pray for this result as you abide in him.

Chapter 10—How Wisdom Trumps Pride and Prejudice

1. Immediately following the Sermon on the Mount (Matthew 5–7), Jesus goes into action. Read Matthew 8:1–17. How did his actions reflect impartiality in ministering to people? What categories of people did he serve? Why might this have been surprising to people of his day? How can you surprise people of this day with your acts of impartiality?
2. Review again James' teaching on impartiality in James 2:1–13. How do you think this could be applied to your own church setting? What can you proactively do to set an example of impartiality? What specifically will this look like in the coming week?

3. Read Romans 12:9–21. How is impartiality demonstrated in these verses? How does this challenge you to be impartial? How can you seek to live this out in the coming week?

Chapter 11—Wise Guys (and Gals) Are the Real Deal

1. Read Matthew 15:1–9. Why did Jesus level these accusations of hypocrisy against the religious leaders of his day? What might cause Jesus to approach modern-day believers in the same way? Is there any need for you to apply this passage to your own life? If so, how? Commit this to him in prayer today.
2. According to the following verses, what are the key ingredients to sincere living? (Philippians 1:10; 1 Timothy 1:5; 2 Timothy 1:5; Hebrews 10:22; 1 Peter 1:22; and 2 Peter 3:1–2.) Based on these verses, what commitment might you embrace in this coming week?
3. Read 2 Samuel 11:1–12:15. What "mask" was David wearing during this dark season of his life to try cover up his hypocrisy? How did God remove the mask? When the mask was removed, what changed? Based on Psalm 51, what key principles can help you live without hypocrisy?

Chapter 12—Reaping Right Relationships

1. Read the parable in Mark 4:1–20. How have you seen these scenarios played out in the lives of people you have known? What can you do to assure that your life will reflect the imagery of verse 20? How might the teaching in James 1:21 help?
2. Read James 1:22–26. Thinking of the analogy of the seed of God's Word and the soil of your heart, what attitude and approach should you take as you read the Bible? As you listen to a sermon? As you read a book of biblical teaching? How will you take this approach as you finish this study?
3. The fruit of righteousness was highlighted by David later in life in Psalm 15:1–2. What do you learn about righteousness

from these two verses? As this chapter stated, "Righteousness is fulfillment of the expectations in any relationship whether with God or other people." How does the rest of Psalm 15 reflect this truth? Which of these relational marks of righteousness do you most need to embrace today?

Notes

Preface

1. Eliza E. Hewitt, "More About Jesus," 1887.

Introduction: Wisdom Within

1. http://www.merriam-webster.com/dictionary/wisdom.
2. David A. Hubbard, quoted in *New Bible Dictionary*, ed. I. Howard Marshall, et al. (Downers Grove, IL: InterVarsity Press, 1996).
3. D. A. Carson, *Teach Us to Pray* (Eugene, OR: Wipf and Stock, 2002), 107–108.
4. Unsigned review of *Acres of Diamonds* by Russell Conwell, Nexus, http://www.coachingforwealth.com.au/articles/book_reviews/acres_of_diamonds_by_russell_conwell/.

Part One: Best Wisdom Available
Chapter 1: Wise Beyond Solomon

1. Arthur Bennett, ed., *The Valley of Vision* (Carlisle, PA: Banner of Truth, 2014), 392.
2. A.W. Tozer, *The Knowledge of the Holy* (New York: Harper and Row, 1961), 68–69.
3. Alleged to have been found on the body of a dead Confederate soldier during the Civil War.
4. "How Rich Was King Solomon?" BibleStudy.org, http://www.Biblestudy.org/basicart/how-rich-was-solomon.html.
5. Solomon received 666 talents of gold each year (1 Kings 10:14). This means the value of what he got each year was between $1,092,906,000 and $1,165,766,400 U.S. dollars.
6. Ibid., "How Rich Was King Solomon?"

7. Walter Elwell, ed., *Baker Encyclopedia of the Bible* (Grand Rapids, MI: Baker Book House, 1988), 1831.

8. David Guzik, "1 Kings 11—Solomon's Decline and Death," Enduring Word, http://www.enduringword.com/commentaries/1111.htm.

9. John MacArthur, *The MacArthur Study Bible* (Nashville: Thomas Nelson, 2006), 865.

10. *Indiana Jones and the Last Crusade*, directed by Steven Spielberg (Hollywood: Paramount Pictures, 1989).

Chapter 2: Accessing Your Wisdom Treasure

1. Arthur Bennett, ed., *The Valley of Vision* (Carlisle, PA: Banner of Truth, 2014), 399.

2. John MacArthur, *James: The MacArthur New Testament Commentary* (Chicago: Moody Press, 1988), 36.

3. Peter Davids, *The Epistle of James, New International Greek Testament Commentary* (Grand Rapids, MI: Eerdmans, 1982), 73.

4. Douglas Moo, *The Letter of James* (Grand Rapids, MI: Eerdmans, 2000), 59.

5. John Calvin and John Owen, *Commentaries on the Catholic Epistles* (Bellingham, WA: Logos Bible Software, 2010), 282.

6. Davids, *The Epistle of James*, 72.

7. Michael Griffiths, *The Example of Jesus* (Downers Grove, IL: InterVarsity Press, 1985), 182.

Chapter 3: The Relational Game Changer

1. Mark Baker, *The Greatest Psychologist Who Ever Lived* (San Francisco: Harper Collins, 2001), 228.

2. Martin Goldsmith, *Jesus and His Relationships* (Carlisle, UK: Paternoster Press, 2000), 1, 4.

3. Rafat Ali, "No Vacation Nation: 41% of Americans Didn't Take a Day Off in 2015," Skift, https://skift.com/2016/01/18/no-vacation-nation-41-of-americans-didnt-take-a-day-off-in-2015/

4. A. T. Robertson, *Word Pictures in the New Testament*—John 1:1 (Nashville, TN: Broadman Press, 1933).

5. Marvin Richardson Vincent, *Word Studies in the New Testament*, vol. 2 (New York: Charles Scribner's Sons, 1887), 35.

6. J. I. Packer, *Knowing God* (Downers Grove, IL: InterVarsity Press, 1973), 97.

7. Francis Schaeffer, *The Mark of the Christian* (Downers Grove, IL: InterVarsity Press, 1970), 8.

8. Ibid., 13.

9. Ibid., 17.

Part Two: Best Wisdom Practices
Chapter 4: Purely Wise in a Wicked World

1. Charles Edward Jefferson, *The Character of Jesus* (1908; repr., New York: Forgotten Books, 2015), 334.

2. William Barclay, *The Letters of James and Peter* (Philadelphia: Westminster Press, 1976), 95.

3. Jerry Bridges, *The Pursuit of Holiness* (Colorado Springs: NavPress, 1978), 46.

4. A.W. Tozer, *The Knowledge of the Holy* (New York: Harper and Row, 1961), 65.

5. Walter Henrichsen, *Thoughts From the Diary of a Desperate Man* (El Cajon, CA: Leadership Foundation, 2011), 364.

Chapter 5: Wisdom Wins in a Culture at War

1. Heidi Jo Fulk, "Ground Your Heart in Gospel Peace," Revive Our Hearts, July 11, 2016, https://www.reviveourhearts.com/true-woman/blog/ground-your-heart-gospel-peace/.

2. F. B. Huey, *Jeremiah, Lamentations,* vol. 16 (Nashville: Broadman and Holman, 1993), 98–99.

3. Thomas Watson, *The Lord's Prayer* (Edinburgh: Banner of Truth, 1999), 12–13.

4. Martin Goldsmith, *Jesus and His Relationships* (Carlisle, UK: Paternoster Press, 2000), 8.

5. Irving Weiss, *Thesaurus of Book Digests, 1950–1980* (New York: Crown Publishing, 1980), 351.

6. Quoted in Ray Ellis, "Wait on the Lord" (sermon, January 25, 2009), http://www.sermoncentral.com/illustrations/sermon-illustration-sermoncentral-staff-stories-godinthehardships-71842.asp.

7. Joseph Scriven, "What a Friend We Have in Jesus," 1855.

8. Priscilla Shirer, *Discerning the Voice of God: How to Recognize When He Speaks* (Chicago: Moody Publishers, 2012), 108.

9. "Story of 'Merchant of Death' Alfred Nobel," *The Swedish Wire*, October 4, 2010, http://www.swedishwire.com/science/6521-story-of-the-merchant-of-death-alfred-nobel.

Chapter 6: Gentle Wisdom—Still in Style

1. Max Lucado, *When God Whispers Your Name* (Nashville: Thomas Nelson, 1994), 73.

2. George W. Bethune, *The Fruit of the Spirit* (Swengel, PA: Reiner Publications, 1839), 100.

3. Walter Elwell, ed., *Evangelical Dictionary of Biblical Theology* (Grand Rapids, MI: Baker Book House, 1996), electronic edition.

4. J. C. Connell, quoted in *New Bible Dictionary*, ed. I. Howard Marshall, et al. (Downers Grove, IL: InterVarsity Press, 1996), 405.

5. Jerry Bridges, *The Practice of Godliness* (Colorado Springs: Navpress, 1984), 221.

6. Billy Graham, *The Holy Spirit* (Waco, TX: Word Books, 1978), 205–206.

7. Bridges, *The Practice of Godliness,* 220,

8. Vine's Expository Dictionary of New Testament Words, http://www2.mf.no/bibelprog/vines.pl?word=Meekness.

9. Ibid.

10. Leon Morris, *The Gospel According to Matthew* (Grand Rapids, MI: Eerdmans, 1992), 98.

11. C. S. Lewis, *Mere Christianity* (New York: Macmillan, 1975), 109–110.

12. A.W. Tozer, *The Knowledge of the Holy* (New York: Harper and Row, 1961), 9.

13. Bill Gaither, "Gentle Shepherd, Come and Lead Us," 1975.

14. Dorothy A. Thrupp, "Savior Like a Shepherd Lead Us," 1836.

15. Nancy DeMoss Wolgemuth, "Developing a Meek Spirit," Revive Our Hearts Radio Broadcast, June 17, 2013, https://www.reviveourhearts.com/radio/revive-our-hearts/developing-meek-spirit/.

16. Jerry Bridges, *Holiness Day by Day* (Colorado Springs: NavPress, 2008).

17. Ibid.

18. Ibid.

19. Aesop, *The North Wind and the Sun* (Sixth Century), http://www.aesopfables.com/cgi/aesop1.cgi?3&TheNorthWindandtheSun.

Chapter 7: Wise Reason for Unreasonable People

1. Michel de Montaigne, *The Complete Essays of Montaigne*, trans. Donald Frame (Palo Alto, CA: Stanford University Press, 1976), 706.

2. John MacArthur, *James: The MacArthur New Testament Commentary* (Chicago: Moody Press, 1998), 179.

3. Michael Griffiths, *The Example of Jesus* (Downers Grove, IL: InterVarsity Press, 1985), 154.

4. *Sayings of the Jewish Fathers (Pirqe Aboth)*, trans. Charles Taylor (Cambridge: Cambridge University Press, 1897), http://www.sacred-texts.com/jud/sjf/sjf07.htm.

5. William Barclay, *The Letters of James and Peter* (Philadelphia: Westminster Press, 1976), 196.

6. G. S. Gates, "An Observational Study of Anger," *Journal of Experimental Psychology*, 9, no. 4 (1926): 325–326.

7. Jay E. Adams, *The Christian Counselor's Manual* (Phillipsburg, PA: Presbyterian and Reformed Publishers, 1963), 350.

8. Peter H. Davids, *The Epistle of James, New International Greek Testament Commentary* (Grand Rapids, MI: Eerdmans, 1982), 254.

Chapter 8: Mercy Me, I'm Getting Wiser!

1. John Piper, *The Pleasures of God* (Portland, OR: Multnomah, 1991), 191.

2. William Barclay, *The Letters of James and Peter* (Philadelphia: Westminster Press, 1976), 96–97.

3. Charles J. Rolls, *His Glorious Name* (Neptune, NJ: Loizeaux Brothers, 1975), 187.

4. A. W. Pink, *The Attributes of God* (Grand Rapids, MI: Baker Books, 1975), 72.

5. Thomas Goodwin, *The Works of Thomas Goodwin, Vol 8: The Object and Acts of Justifying Faith* (Edinburgh: Banner of Truth, 1985), 25.

6. Tim Challies, "God's Mercy and God's Wrath Meet at the Cross," Informing the Reformed, August 16, 2012, http://www.challies.com/articles/gods-mercy-and-gods-wrath-meet-at-the-cross.

7. Martin Goldsmith, *Jesus and His Relationships* (Carlisle, UK: Paternoster Press, 2000), 56.

8. John MacArthur, "Happy Are the Merciful," Grace to You, 2016, https://www.gty.org/resources/print/sermons/2202.

9. William Newell, "At Calvary" (1895).

10. Isaac Watts, "Alas! And Did My Savior Bleed?" (1707).

11. Metropolitan Anthony Bloom, "The Jesus Prayer," http://www.orthodoxchristian.info/pages/Jprayer.html, quoted in Metropolitan Anthony Bloom, *Living Faith* (Springfield, IL: Temlegate, 1966), 84–88.

Chapter 9: How the Good Die Wise

1. It should be noted that although this saying is traditionally known as John Wesley's Rule, there is no evidence he actually said it.

2. A. W. Pink, *The Attributes of God* (Grand Rapids. MI: Baker Books, 1975), 57.

3. "Sermon LXXVII," Christian Classics Ethereal Library, http://www.ccel.org/ccel/manton/manton07.xxv.html.

4. Charles Spurgeon, "The Treasury of David" (Psalm 118), The Spurgeon Archive, http://www.spurgeon.org/treasury/ps118.php.

5. Nancy DeMoss Wolgemuth, "Is God Really Good?" Revive Our Hearts Radio Broadcast, January 15, 2013, https://www.reviveourhearts.com/radio/revive-our-hearts/god-really-good/.

6. Timothy Keller, quoted in Bruce Hurt, "Poiema—God's Workmanship," *Preceptaustin*, September 22, 2015, https://preceptaustin.wordpress.com/2015/09/22/poiema-gods-workmanship/.

7. John Piper, *The Pleasures of God* (Portland, OR: Multnomah, 1991), 197–199.

8. For information on *The Deeper Life*, go to http://bakerpublishinggroup.com/books/the-deeper-life/348150 and consider the small-group study here: http://www.strategicrenewal.com/value-packs/the-deeper-life-group-study/.

9. One line in my theology statement reads: "My God is completely *good*. Even when circumstances and people seem bad, he is at work with my best interests in mind."

10. My personal identity statement reads: "I, Daniel D. Henderson, am a new creature in Jesus Christ—a completely loved, fully accepted, and totally empowered child of the most *good*, most high, most holy God. I have been created by his amazing grace for life full of *good* works and God's glory through Christ my Lord."

11. Spurgeon, "The Treasury of David" (Psalm 118).

12. Tyler Smith, "In Memory of Elisabeth Elliot: 30 of Her Most Inspiring Quotes," *LogosTalk*, June 15, 2015, https://blog.logos.com/2015/06/in-memory-of-elisabeth-elliot-30-of-her-most-inspiring-quotes/.

13. George Mueller, *Autobiography of George Mueller*, comp. G. Fred Bergin (London: J. Nisbet, 1906), 424.

14. Piper, *Pleasures of God*, 188.

15. Ibid., 189.

Chapter 10: How Wisdom Trumps Pride and Prejudice

1. John Piper, "There Is No Partiality With God, Part 1" (Sermon, December 27, 1998), http://www.desiringgod.org/messages/there-is-no-partiality-with-god-part-1.

2. Marjorie Wallace, *The Silent Twins* (New York: Prentice Hall, 1986).

3. Oliver Sacks, "Bound Together in Fantasy and Crime," *New York Times*, October 19, 1986, http://www.nytimes.com/1986/10/19/books/bound-together-in-fantasy-and-crime.html.

4. John Piper, "There Is No Partiality With God, Part 1."

5. Peter Davids, *The Epistle of James, New International Greek Commentary* (Grand Rapids, MI: Eerdmans, 1982), 154–155.

6. John MacArthur, *James: The MacArthur New Testament Commentary* (Chicago: Moody Press, 1988), 113.

7. Michael Griffiths, *The Example of Jesus* (Downers Grove, IL: InterVarsity Press, 1985), 130.

Chapter 11: Wise Guys (and Gals) Are the Real Deal

1. David Hubbard, *The Book of James: Wisdom That Works* (Waco, TX: Word Books, 1980), 84.

2. Henry Young, "Lance Armstrong: He Was a 'Tragic Hero,'" CNN, April 12, 2016, http://edition.cnn.com/2016/04/12/sport/lance-armstrong-david-walsh-stephen-frears-the-program-cycling/.

3. Ibid.

4. Ibid.

5. Charles Edward Jefferson, *The Character of Jesus* (1908; repr., New York: Forgotten Books, 2015), 57.

6. Douglas Moo, *The Letter of James* (Grand Rapids, MI: Eerdmans, 2000), 177.

7. Peter Davids, *The Epistle of James, New International Greek Testament Commentary* (Grand Rapids, MI: Eerdmans, 1982), 154–155.

8. Jefferson, *The Character of Jesus*, 58.

9. Ibid., 58.

10. M. R. DeHaan, "Hypocrites," April 17, 2001, *Our Daily Bread* (devotional), April 17, 2001, http://odb.org/2001/04/17/hypocrites/.

11. This is covered in depth in my book *The Deeper Life: Satisfying the 8 Vital Longings of Your Soul* (Minneapolis: Bethany House, 2014), 147–163.

12. Walter A. Henrichsen, *Thoughts From the Diary of a Desperate Man* (El Cajon, CA: Leadership Foundation, 2011), Day 266.

Chapter 12: Reaping Right Relationships

1. John MacArthur, *James: The MacArthur New Testament Commentary* (Chicago: Moody Press, 1998), 180.

2. William Barclay, *The Letters of James and Peter* (Philadelphia: Westminster Press, 1976), 97.

3. Tuvia Teldon, "The Power of the Seed," http://www.chabad.org/parshah/article_cdo/aid/911728/jewish/The-Power-of-the-Seed.htm.

4. Mehmet Oz, "The Power of Seeds," *The Dr. Oz Show*, January 21, 2010, http://www.doctoroz.com/videos/power-seeds.

5. MacArthur, *James*, 180.

6. Duane Garrett, *Proverbs, Ecclesiastes, Song of Songs: The New American Commentary* (Nashville: Broadman and Holman, 1993), 75–76.

7. Walter Elwell, ed., *Baker Encyclopedia of the Bible* (Grand Rapids, MI: Baker Book House, 1988), 1860.

8. Ibid.

9. Ibid.

10. M. G. Easton, *Easton's Bible Dictionary* (New York: Harper and Brothers, 1893).

11. Michael Griffiths, *The Example of Jesus* (Downers Grove, IL: InterVarsity Press, 1985), 184.

12. MacArthur, *James*, 180.

13. G. Walter Hansen, *The Letter to the Philippians* (Grand Rapids, MI: Eerdmans, 2009), 171.

Conclusion: Daily Delight and Dependence

1. Douglas Moo, *The Letter of James* (Grand Rapids, MI: Eerdmans, 2000), 174.

2. Arthur Bennett, ed., *The Valley of Vision* (Carlisle, PA: Banner of Truth, 2014), 147.

3. Walter A. Henrichsen, *Thoughts From the Diary of a Desperate Man* (El Cajon, CA: Leadership Foundation, 2011), Day 194.

4. Ibid.

Appendix 1: Jesus' Model of Prayer

1. Derek Thomas, *Praying the Saviour's Way* (Fearn, UK: Christian Focus Publications, 2002), 43.

2. Robert Law, *The Tests of Life* (Edinburgh: T&T Clark, 1909), 304.

3. Warren Wiersbe, *On Earth as it Is in Heaven: How the Lord's Prayer Teaches Us to Pray More Effectively* (Grand Rapids, MI: Baker Books, 2010), 68.

4. Ibid., 91.

Application and Discussion Questions

1. Thomas Watson, *The Lord's Prayer* (Edinburgh: Banner of Truth, 1999), 12–13.

For almost three decades, **Daniel Henderson**, was a pastor to thousands in congregations in California and Minnesota. He serves as founder and president of Strategic Renewal International (www.strategicrenewal.com) and is also the national director for The 6:4 Fellowship (www.64fellowship.com). As a "pastor to pastors," Daniel leads renewal events in local churches, speaks in a variety of leadership conferences, and coaches leaders across North America. Daniel is the author of ten books. He and his wife, Rosemary, live near Moneta, Virgina.

STRATEGIC RENEWAL

TRANSFORMING PRAYER

It's no wonder so many people are discouraged with prayer. Instead of a genuine encounter with God, our prayers are often limited to a grocery list of requests. But there is a difference between seeking His provisions and seeking His face. Discover how to awaken your prayer life and experience the life-changing power of worship-based prayer.

THE DEEPER LIFE

Satisfy your soul! Learn how to identify the vital longings of your soul, and discover the keys to satisfying them daily. This gospel-oriented approach will guide you, step-by-step, out of the fog of constant distractions and into an intentional life of purpose and transformation.

TRANSFORMING PRESENCE

We sing songs about Him. We've seen His name in the Bible. And most of us know He's a part of the Trinity, but misunderstandings, confusion, and contention abound. And it's keeping us from the abundant, satisfying life God has for us. Discover the transformational, personal, and joyful relationship that comes from meeting the Holy Spirit on His own terms.

Join us every monday on Facebook LIVE, as we engage in Scripture-fed, Spirit-led, Worship-based prayer together! On Facebook @strategicrenewal

Get daily encouragement! Discipleship Daily is a simple, short thought and scripture per day through the Strategic Renewal app. Available free from iTunes, GooglePlay and the Amazon App Store.

Are you a pastor? Do you long for others who understand what you're going through? Then The 6:4 Fellowship is the place for you. It's a place where you can find like-minded conviction, community and capacity to do the ministry God has called you to do.

www.ingramcontent.com/pod-product-compliance
Lightning Source LLC
LaVergne TN
LVHW010611100826
845148LV00014B/2921

* 9 7 9 8 9 8 6 2 8 6 1 2 9 *